Dale,
another year!

Blessings,

A knowledge resource from The Masters Program

THE LAW OF REWARDS

THE LAW OF REWARDS

✢ ✢ ✢ ✢ ✢ ✢

RANDY ALCORN

A Generous Giving book
published by

TYNDALE HOUSE PUBLISHERS, INC.
CAROL STREAM, ILLINOIS

Visit Tyndale's exciting Web site at www.tyndale.com

TYNDALE is a registered trademark of Tyndale House Publishers, Inc.

Tyndale's quill logo is a trademark of Tyndale House Publishers, Inc.

The Law of Rewards

Designed by Jenny Swanson

Portions of this work were originally published in *Money, Possessions, and Eternity,* copyright © 1989, 2002 by Eternal Perspective Ministries. All rights reserved. Revised and updated 2003.

Library of Congress Cataloging-in-Publication Data

Alcorn, Randy C.
    The law of rewards : giving what you can't keep to gain what you can't lose / Randy Alcorn.
        p. cm.
Portions of this work were originally published in Money, possessions, and eternity. c1989.
Includes bibliographical references.
    ISBN-13: 978-0-8423-8106-2 (hc)
    ISBN-10: 0-8423-8106-6 (hc)
    1. Wealth—Religious aspects—Christianity.   I. Alcorn, Randy C.
Money, possessions, and eternity.   II. Title.
BR115.W4 A435 2003
48'.6—dc12   2003001352

Printed in the United States of America

09   08   07   06
7   6   5   4   3

CONTENTS

To Kathy Norquist, Bonnie Hiestand, Janet Albers, and Sharon Misenhimer. Nanci and I are deeply grateful for your help and friendship.

WHY THIS BOOK?

My book *Money, Possessions, and Eternity,* a practical theology of money, was first published in 1989. It contains five chapters centered on eternal rewards.

At that time rewards were rarely discussed by evangelicals—and almost never in relationship to stewardship and giving. Yet I believed rewards were a central part of stewardship, and that a biblical study of money and possessions would be incomplete without addressing this subject.

Over the years people have remarked to me how much they were challenged and enlightened by these five chapters. But often they've lamented, "This treatment of rewards is buried in the middle of a big book, and most people will never read it." Unfortunately, they're right. The rewards chapters are really a book within a book. They will be discovered only by those undertaking the study of a theology of money, which deals with many other issues.

I suggested to my friends at Generous Giving and Tyndale House Publishers that the subject of rewards might warrant a book of its own. That's what *The Law of Rewards* is—a thoroughly revised version of some of what I addressed in *Money, Possessions, and Eternity.* I have tailored my original writings for the distinctive purposes of this book, then integrated some new material I've written that strengthens and rounds it out.

The Law of Rewards will serve the church as a stand-alone biblical study focused squarely on eternal rewards—with special emphasis on giving as an eternal investment.

I hope you enjoy this book as much as I have enjoyed writing and speaking on giving and eternal rewards.

If you wish to view rewards in the larger context of financial stewardship, I recommend you read the entire *Money, Possessions, and Eternity* (which I thoroughly revised and updated in 2003). In addition to its much larger format, the revised version has subject and Scripture indices that help the reader explore nearly every aspect of the biblical doctrine of stewardship. It also has a study and discussion guide in the back, for group use.

Now settle into *The Law of Rewards* to take a close look at a subject of vast importance, long neglected and misunderstood by evangelical Christians.

By God's sovereign grace, may we eagerly invest in eternity, joyfully giving what we cannot keep to gain what we cannot lose.

Randy Alcorn

NOT DIVESTING
BUT INVESTING

What's the biggest misconception Christians have about giving? That when we give money away to a church or ministry, or to help the needy, it's gone. While we hope others will benefit from it, we're quite sure *we* won't. We think we're *divesting* ourselves of money, disassociating from it. Once it leaves our hands, we imagine, it has no connection to us, no future implications relevant to our lives.

We couldn't be more wrong.

What we think we own will be rudely taken from us—some of it before we die, and anything that's left the moment we die. But now is our window of opportunity not to *divest* ourselves of money but to *invest* it in heaven. We don't have to have everything taken from us. We can give it before disaster or death strike. Now's our chance to give what we can't keep to gain what we can't lose.

We are God's money managers. He wants us to invest his money in his kingdom. He tells us he's keeping track of every cup of cold water we give the needy in his name. He promises us he will reward us in heaven because we help the poor and needy who cannot pay us back for what we do for them.

We can buy up shares in God's kingdom. We can invest in eternity.

HY GIVING IS BETTER THAN RECEIVING

When Jesus said, "It is more blessed to give than to receive" (Acts 20:35), he really meant it. It sounds counterintuitive, doesn't it? But when you give, you plug into God's law of rewards. You experience dramatic and lasting returns for the investments you've made. When you give, you receive far more than when you keep.

When you give, therefore, it is not only for the glory of God and the good of others—though those would certainly be good enough reasons. When you give, it is for *your* good too.

This morning a man called me because he wants to give away as much as he can to God's kingdom. He's normally not bubbly, but his voice rang with passion. He was far more excited than if he had been talking about buying a new car. Through giving, he was getting something far better—something that wouldn't rust or get totaled or lose its appeal. He talked to me about wanting to please God and receive eternal rewards. He believed that through his giving he was getting something far more valuable than anything he could acquire on earth—something that will be waiting for him when he gets to heaven.

Some would think he's foolish to talk this way. But I'm convinced he's absolutely right.

I spend a lot of time talking with givers. At one gathering, we went around the room and told our giving stories. I took notes. The most common words used to describe giving were "joy," "fun," "exciting," and "wonderful." There were lots of smiles and laughter, even tears of joy. One older couple shared how they travel around the world getting involved in the missions work they support. Meanwhile their house in

California is getting run down. They said, "Our children keep telling us, 'Fix up your house, or buy a new one. You can afford it!' We tell them, 'Why would we do that? That's not what excites us!' "

Many Christians don't give. Others determine to do their part but sigh deeply before writing a check to their church or ministry. They give strictly out of a sense of duty and obligation. Better to give out of duty than not give at all, but how sad to miss out on the joy. That joy comes when you understand God's law of rewards.

What's the difference between reluctant and joyful givers? Reluctant givers give as if they were spending and getting nothing in return. Joyful givers give as if they were investing, anticipating a great deal in return. Those who "get it" understand the law of rewards and are infused with purpose. Those who don't get it don't know what they're missing . . . and what they're missing is something truly great.

When they hand over money, investors don't say to themselves, "I'll never see this again; I'll never benefit from it." No. The reason they invest is because they not only believe in what they're doing but are also anticipating eventual benefits that will come back to them: rewards.

THE REWARD CONNECTION

Most Christians have heard about eternal rewards, but many consider them to be figurative—nice words about crowns, but come on, who wants a crown anyway? A chalet in the mountains, a new boat, golfing on the finest courses and going to the Bahamas . . . doesn't that sound like a lot more fun? Why wait for something later that doesn't sound so great anyway?

This is one of our problems. We forget earth is not our home, so we waste our lives pouring ourselves and our money into what will go up in smoke. Meanwhile, God offers us the opportunity to experience a down payment of joy—the delight that comes *today* in doing what you know God wants, and anticipating hearing him say to you *tomorrow,* "Well done."

Too often we think of heavenly rewards as unconnected to our earthly actions. In fact, they are tangible dividends we can gain by the things we do and say on earth.

As we'll make clear later, this isn't salvation by works; faith in Jesus is our one and *only* basis for entering heaven. But the Bible shows that while our faith determines our eternal destination, our behavior—including what we do with our money—determines our eternal rewards.

In this book we'll talk about how we can honor God with our money, what actions and attitudes God rewards, what eternal rewards are, and why it's okay—and, in fact, *important*—to be motivated by them. We'll see that giving isn't about trying harder to do the right thing while quietly resenting our sacrifices. It's about understanding how God made us

and responding joyfully to the way he motivates us. It's about seeing what God is doing and eagerly buying up shares. (Who wants to be left out of the world's greatest investment opportunity?)

Let's open our minds to truths of Scripture that lay buried beneath this culture's rocky surface. Let's discover together the life-changing, eternity-impacting paradigm shift offered us in *the law of rewards.*

CHAPTER 1

WHAT DETERMINES OUR REWARDS?

Jesus Christ said more about money than about any other single thing because, when it comes to a man's real nature, money is of first importance. Money is an exact index to a man's true character. All through Scripture there is an intimate correlation between the development of a man's character and how he handles his money.

RICHARD HALVERSON

A POOR WOMAN AND A RICH MAN

Imagine you're a financial counselor. Today you have two appointments, first with an elderly woman and then a middle-aged man.

The woman's husband died six years ago. She says, "I have no more money. The cupboards are bare. These two dollars are all I have to live on, yet I feel as if God wants me to put them in the offering. What do you think?"

What would you tell her?

Likely you'd say, "That's very generous of you, but God gave you common sense. He knows your heart—that you want to give. But he intends you to take care of yourself. I'm sure God would have you keep those two dollars and buy food for tomorrow. You can't

1

IF CHRIST IS NOT
LORD OVER OUR
MONEY AND
POSSESSIONS,
THEN HE IS NOT
OUR LORD.

expect him just to send down food from heaven, can you? God wants us to be sensible."

Your next appointment is with a successful, hardworking, middle-aged farmer whose crop production has been excellent. He tells you, "I'm planning to tear down my old barns to build bigger ones so I can store up more crops and goods and have plenty saved up for the future. Then I can take it easy, retire early, and do some traveling and golfing. What do you think?"

How would you answer?

Perhaps like this: "Sounds good to me! You've worked hard. God has blessed you with good crops. It's your business, your crops, your money. If you can save up enough to take care of yourself the rest of your life, by all means go for it. I hope one day I'll be in a position to do the same!"

Wouldn't such advice to this poor widow and rich man appear reasonable? What would God have to say about it?

We needn't speculate—Scripture tells us *exactly* what he says.

In Mark 12 we meet a poor widow. She put two tiny copper coins in the temple offering box. This was the only money she had. Jesus pointed her out to his disciples to teach them a lesson. Did he question the woman's wisdom? Did he say she should have been more sensible than to surrender her only remaining resources? No. He gave her unqualified commendation: "I tell you the truth, this poor widow has put more into the treasury than all the others. They all gave out of their wealth; but she, out of her poverty, put in everything—all she had to live on" (Mark 12:43-44).

Jesus regarded the woman as wise, not foolish. He set her up as a model for his disciples to follow. He enshrined her example in the Word of God so that future generations might emulate her faith and sacrificial generosity.

And yet, if she'd come to us for advice, we would have tried to talk her out of doing the very thing that Jesus commended her for!

In Luke 12 we meet a rich man. We're not told that he gained his wealth dishonestly or that he didn't attend synagogue, tithe, or pray, as most Jews did. He worked diligently to build his business. Now, like any good businessman, he wanted to expand by building bigger barns. His purpose was to accumulate enough wealth to retire early and have a good time. Sounds like the American dream, doesn't it? (And, honestly, are our dreams as Christians so different?)

So what did God have to say to this man? "You fool! This very night your life will be demanded from you. Then who will get what you have prepared for yourself?"

Jesus added, "This is how it will be with anyone who stores up things for himself but is not rich toward God" (Luke 12:20-21).

By our standards, the widow's actions seem unwise and the rich man's seem wise. But God, who knows the hearts of both and sees from the vantage point of eternity, regards the poor woman as eternally wise and the rich man as eternally foolish.

This proves that our beliefs about money are radically different from God's. In fact, they're diametrically opposed.

We must ask some probing questions. Who is featured more frequently in Christian magazines and on talk shows—poor widows or rich fools? Who receives the most respect and attention in many Christian organizations? Who is more highly esteemed in most churches? Who typically serves on our boards and determines the direction of our ministries?

Let's be honest—don't we have a scarcity of poor widows and a surplus of rich fools? And doesn't our way of operating encourage people to think and act like the rich fool, and discourage them from thinking and acting like the poor widow?

THE STORY MONEY TELLS

Jesus did not and does not call *all* his disciples to give away their last pennies. But he also knows that none of us can enthrone the true God unless in the process we dethrone our other gods. If Christ is not Lord over our money and possessions, then he is not our Lord. The principle is timeless: There is a powerful relationship between our true spiritual condition and our attitude and actions concerning money and possessions.

The early church exemplifies this connection. The depth of transformation in the early Christians was clearly evident in their willingness to surrender their money and possessions to meet each others' needs (Acts 2:44-45; 4:32-35). It was no more natural for these Christians to cheerfully liquidate and disburse assets they had spent their lives accumulating than it would be for us. And that's the whole point. Conversion and the filling of the Holy Spirit are *super*natural experiences that produce supernatural responses— whether in the first century or the twenty-first. Although private ownership of property was still practiced by the early Christians, the joyful giving and sharing of this property became the new norm of supernatural living.

A study of the early church, the poor widow, the rich fool, Zacchaeus, the rich young ruler, and many other Bible characters shows that our handling of money is a litmus test of our true character. It's an index of our spiritual life. Our stewardship of our money and possessions becomes the story of our lives.

If this is true of all people in all ages, doesn't it have a special application to us who live in a time and place of unparalleled affluence? who live in a country where the "poverty level" exceeds the average standard of living of nearly every other society in human history, past or present?

If you have sufficient food, decent clothes, live in a home that shields you from the weather, and own some kind of reliable transportation, you're in the top 15 percent of the world's wealthy. Add some savings, two cars (in any condition), a variety of clothes, and your own house, and you have reached the top 5 percent. You may not feel wealthy, but that's only because you're comparing yourself to the mega-wealthy.

GOD'S WORDS AS A GUIDE

Scripture contains many verses that give guidance on money. In these sidebars throughout the book we'll highlight some that may help you as you rethink your attitude toward giving and rewards.

"The earth is the Lord's, and everything in it, the world, and all who live in it." (Psalm 24:1)

"You may say to yourself, 'My power and the strength of my hands have produced this wealth for me.' But remember the Lord your God, for it is he who gives you the ability to produce wealth, and so confirms his covenant, which he swore to your forefathers." (Deuteronomy 8:17-18)

Consider someone who works from age twenty-five to sixty-five and makes only $25,000 a year. Forget the huge value of benefits provided, interest earned, pay raises, and other income sources, including inheritance or Social Security. Even without these extras, in his lifetime this person of modest income will be paid a *million* dollars. He will manage a fortune.

Because we all will eventually give an account of our lives to God (Romans 14:12; 2 Corinthians 5:10), one day everyone must answer these questions: Where did it all go? What did I spend it on? What, if anything, did I support with it? What has been accomplished for eternity through my use of all this wealth?

We will be held accountable for what we do in this life, including what we do with our money. If we are generous with our possessions and faithful in our service, God will reward us beyond our imagination! If we live only for ourselves, hoarding our money and focusing on our earthly comfort, we will lose the eternal rewards God had planned for us. As Christians, we are saved by God's grace—but what we do in this life will matter for eternity.

THIS IS THE LAW OF REWARDS:
WHILE OUR FAITH DETERMINES
OUR ETERNAL DESTINATION,
OUR BEHAVIOR DETERMINES
OUR ETERNAL REWARDS.

In the account of the poor widow, Mark writes, "Jesus sat down opposite the place where the offerings were put and watched the crowd putting their money into the temple treasury" (Mark 12:41). Notice that it doesn't say, "Jesus happened to see . . ." No, he deliberately *watched* to observe what people were giving.

How close was Jesus to the offering box? Close enough to see that some people put in large amounts. Close enough even to see two tiny coins in a shriveled old hand and to identify them as copper. Jesus was interested enough in what people were giving to make an object lesson for his disciples.

This passage should make all of us who suppose that what we do with our money is our own business feel terribly uncomfortable. It's painfully apparent that God considers it *his* business. He does not apologize for watching with intense interest what we do with the money he's entrusted to us. If we use our imagination, we might peer into the invisible realm to see him gathering some of his subjects together this very moment. Perhaps you can hear him using your handling of finances as an object lesson.

The question is this: What kind of example are you?

LEARNING ABOUT GOD'S OWNERSHIP

In 1990 I was a pastor and on the board of a pregnancy resource center. After searching the Scriptures and praying, I began participating in nonviolent rescues at abortion clinics. I was arrested several times and went to jail for a couple of days. An abortion clinic subsequently won a court judgment against me and others. I told the judge that normally I would pay anything I owed, but I couldn't hand over money to people who would use it to kill babies.

Soon after, I discovered that my church was about to receive a writ of garnishment, demanding that they surrender one-fourth of my wages each month to the abortion clinic. The church would either have to pay the abortion clinic or defy a court order. To avoid this, I had to resign. The only way I could prevent garnishment in the future was to make no more than minimum wage.

Another court judgment followed, involving another abortion clinic. We were assessed the largest judgment ever against a group of peaceful protestors: $8.4 million. By all appearances, our lives had taken a devastating turn—but it was one of the best things that ever happened to us.

What others intended for evil, God intended for good (Genesis 50:20). We began Eternal Perspective Ministries, which owns all the books I write. Nanci worked at a secretary's salary, supplementing my minimum wage. Then something interesting happened: Suddenly my books were on the best-seller lists. Royalties increased. Our ministry has been able to give away 100 percent of those royalties to missions, famine relief, and pro-life work. In the past three years, by God's grace, the ministry has given away more than $500,000. Sometimes I think God sells the books just to raise funds for ministries close to his heart!

I don't go to bed at night feeling that I've "sacrificed" that money, wishing somehow I could get my hands on it. I go to bed feeling joy, because there's nothing like giving.

If you wonder why God has blessed your business, maybe it's not because the goods and services

RANDY ALCORN

you offer are so extraordinary. Maybe it's because he wants to provide you with more money to give back to him, and more reward in heaven! And if you don't realize that, you'll never experience the joy of giving, the thrill of kingdom investing he desires for you.

PATHWAY TO SPIRITUAL GROWTH

I wasn't raised in a Christian home, but from the day I came to Christ as a high school student, giving has been an integral part of my walk with God. Many of the greatest joys of my life, and some of the closest times of intimacy with my Lord, have come in giving. When I become aware of a need and God leads me to give, suddenly I'm infused with energy, purpose, and joy.

Go back to what Jesus said: "It is more blessed to give than to receive" (Acts 20:35). Why? Perhaps because when we give it blesses not one but three parties—God, the recipient, and us. We shouldn't be content with the first blessing, which is when we receive money from God. There is the second blessing of our giving so that others receive, and the third blessing of God being pleased. It is the second and third blessings that keep the first blessing from becoming a curse of having too much, and centering our lives around money and things.

Ironically, the blessing on us when we give money is always greater than if we had kept it. (This is part of God's law of rewards.)

REWARD PRINCIPLE #1: GIVING BRINGS GREATER BLESSING THAN RECEIVING.

By not giving, we don't just rob God or rob others of blessing. We rob ourselves of the rewards God wants to give us.

How many blessings have we kept from ourselves in the last year by failing to give as we could have? How much spiritual growth and joy have we missed out on by not living by God's law of rewards?

For my wife and me, the process of discovering God's will about money and possessions has been exciting and liberating. Our growth in financial stewardship has closely paralleled our overall spiritual growth. In fact, it has propelled it. We have learned more about faith, trust, grace, commitment, and God's provision in this area than any other.

I have also learned why Paul said, "God loves a cheerful giver" (2 Corinthians 9:7). I have found that cheerful givers love God and love him more deeply each time they give. To me, one of the few experiences comparable to the joy of leading someone to Christ is the joy of making wise and generous eternity-impacting choices with my money and possessions. Both are supreme acts of worship. Both are exhilarating. Both are what we were made for.

This book addresses what eternity holds for us and how that relates to our money. I believe this is the primary missing ingredient in most Christian books on finances. When we look at money only as money, and not in light of its potential impact on eternity, we walk away with a shortsighted vision that results in shortsighted financial decisions and lifestyles.

As we look at some of Jesus' teachings about finances, I hope you'll gain clearer vision—of the importance of living for eternity, of the types and extent of eternal rewards, and of the way God created us to be motivated by rewards. When you grasp the concept of delayed gratification in light of eternal rewards, your attitude toward giving will never be the same.

My hope is that even if you have come to this book as a spectator, you will finish it as a participant. I pray you will join a multitude of God's people, past and present, in not just talking about God's grace but also experiencing it at your heart's deepest level.

As we explore together the exciting issues ahead, let's determine not to be rich fools disguised as disciples. Instead, let's develop the heart of the poor widow, learning boldly to put all our resources at God's disposal, as he has put all his resources at ours.

On the wall of President Lyndon Johnson's White House office hung a framed letter written by General Sam Houston to Johnson's great-grandfather Baines more than a hundred years earlier. Baines had led Sam Houston to Christ. Houston was a changed man, no longer coarse and belligerent but peaceful and content.

The day came for Houston to be baptized—an incredible event for those who knew him. After his baptism Houston offered to pay half the local minister's salary. When someone asked him why, he said, "My pocketbook was baptized too."

Sam Houston demonstrated the reality of God's grace to him by reciprocating that grace through giving.

As Sam Houston did, may we learn together the truth that Martin Luther recognized when he said that for each of us there must be not only the conversion of the heart and mind but also the conversion of the purse.

CHAPTER 2

FIREPROOFING OUR MONEY

I have held many things in my hands and I have lost them all. But whatever I have placed in God's hands, that I still possess.
MARTIN LUTHER

In the greatest message ever preached, Jesus addressed the believer's proper relationship to money and possessions:

> Do not store up for yourselves treasures on earth, where moth and rust destroy, and where thieves break in and steal. But store up for yourselves treasures in heaven, where moth and rust do not destroy, and where thieves do not break in and steal. For where your treasure is, there your heart will be also.
>
> The eye is the lamp of the body. If your eyes are good, your whole body will be full of light. But if your eyes are bad, your whole body will be full of darkness. If then the light within you is darkness, how great is that darkness!
>
> No one can serve two masters. Either he will hate the one and love the other, or he will be devoted to the one and despise the other. You

cannot serve both God and Money.
(Matthew 6:19-24)

Jesus always had two kingdoms in mind. He spoke here of the two treasuries, two perspectives, and two masters of those two kingdoms.

Each couplet presents two options and demands one choice. There's a default choice if no choice is made. Unless the right choice is deliberately made and tenaciously clung to, the wrong choice will naturally be implemented. In that case, as if on automatic pilot, people will spend their lives investing in the wrong treasury, adopting the wrong perspective, and serving the wrong master.

TWO TREASURIES

What is our treasure? A. W. Tozer suggested we may discover the answer by responding to four basic questions:

+ What do we value most?
+ What would we most hate to lose?
+ What do our thoughts turn to most frequently when we are free to think of what we will?
+ What affords us the greatest pleasure?[1]

Based on your answers to these four questions, what's *your* treasure?

Many would list people and relationships as their treasures. But if we're honest, we'd also include money and possessions. However, by juxtaposing the storing up of treasures on earth with treasures in heaven, Jesus reveals an eternal use for money and possessions. Instead of viewing them as an end, we should view them as a means to an end. Though they are treasures that will perish, they can be used now—

CHRIST'S PRIMARY ARGUMENT AGAINST AMASSING MATERIAL WEALTH ISN'T THAT IT'S MORALLY WRONG, BUT SIMPLY THAT IT'S A POOR INVESTMENT.

before they perish—to acquire greater treasures that will last forever.

Moths destroy fabric, rust destroys precious metals, and thieves can steal anything. Jesus could have gone on—fires consume, floods destroy, governments seize, enemies attack, investments go sour. No earthly treasure is safe. In fact, God says this present earth will be consumed by fire (2 Peter 3:10). All its treasures will go up in flames. Paul says the fire of God's holiness will consume whatever we've done that amounts to wood, hay, and straw. But he tells us there's something that will survive the fire and go right into the new heavens and new earth—works of gold, silver, and precious stones (1 Corinthians 3:12).

When money and possessions are invested in heavenly treasure rather than earthly, the equation changes radically. The investment takes on eternal value.

Since God, his Word, and people are eternal, what will last is what is used wisely for God, his Word, and his people.

Jesus invites us to choose our treasury. Will we invest our treasures on earth and lose them when we die? Or will we invest our treasures in heaven, where they will be ours for eternity?

If you think about it, there's only one smart choice.

AGGRESSIVE INVESTING

In reading Matthew 6, many people see the negative and miss the positive. They think that Jesus is categorically against the storing up of treasures. In fact, Jesus didn't tell us not to store up treasures. On the contrary, he *commanded* us to store up treasures. He simply said, "Stop storing them up in the wrong place, and start storing them up in the right place."

Christ's primary argument against amassing material wealth isn't that it's morally wrong but simply that it's a poor investment. Material things just won't stand the test of time. Even if they escape moths and rust and thieves, they cannot escape that coming fire of God that will consume the material world.

Jesus isn't saying it's wrong to invest. He's saying, "Don't make a stupid investment; make a smart one."

John Wesley said, "I value all things only by the price they shall gain in eternity."

David Livingstone said, "I place no value on anything I possess, except in relation to the kingdom of God."

God's kingdom was the reference point for these men. They saw all else in light of that kingdom. They were compelled to live as they did, not because they treasured no things, but because they treasured the right things.

Consider missionary martyr Jim Elliot's words, on which I've based the subtitle of this book: "He is no fool who gives what he cannot keep to gain what he cannot lose." People often think of Elliot as one of those superspiritual missionary types who might be described as "unconcerned about gain." But they couldn't be more wrong. We focus on his willingness to sacrifice and serve, but we overlook his passion for personal gain. In fact, that's what his famous words are all about! Reread them and you'll see that *Jim Elliot was seeking gain!* What separated him from the common Christian wasn't that he didn't want gain, but that *he wanted gain that would last.*

GOD'S WORDS AS A GUIDE

"But who am I, and who are my people, that we should be able to give as generously as this? Everything comes from you, and we have given you only what comes from your hand." (1 Chronicles 29:14)

"You will be made rich in every way so that you can be generous on every occasion, and through us your generosity will result in thanksgiving to God." (2 Corinthians 9:11)

Christ's position on wealth is not that it should be rejected but that it should be pursued. It's an understatement to say that God doesn't object to an investment mentality. According to this passage, God *has* an investment mentality. Christ agrees wholeheartedly with us: wealth is worth seeking. The question is, what constitutes true and lasting wealth? And how can we obtain it?

DISCOVERING TRUE WEALTH

Jesus described what it's like when we discover true wealth: "The kingdom of heaven is like treasure hidden in a field. When a man found it, he hid it again, and then in his joy went and sold all he had and bought that field" (Matthew 13:44).

This man, like most of us, was probably quite attached to his possessions. Yet, having seen the value of this great treasure in the field, he "sold all he had" to obtain it. Did the sacrifice pain him? Should we feel sorry for him that the treasure cost him everything? No! "In his joy," he sold all to obtain the treasure. Why? It was a simple question of relative value. Until he found the treasure, all his possessions seemed valuable. But compared to the dazzling beauty and incalculable worth of what he had discovered, everything he had owned and treasured to that point seemed worthless.

John White said this about the man in the parable:

> The choice he faces lies between his worthless bits and pieces and the field with buried treasure. There is nothing noble about his sacrifice. There would, on the other hand, be something incredibly stupid about not making it. Anyone

but a fool would do exactly as the man did.
Everyone will envy him his good fortune and
commend him not on his spiritual character
but on his common sense.[2]

The greatest treasure is Christ himself. To Paul,
gaining Christ made everything else seem compara-
tively worthless (Philippians 3:7-11). But the rewards
God promises us are treasures too, and he expects us
to want them. Christ offers us the incredible opportunity to trade temporary goods and currency for
eternal rewards. By putting our money and possessions in his treasury while we're still on earth, we
assure ourselves of vastly greater eternal rewards
in heaven.

**REWARD PRINCIPLE #2: WHEN WE INVEST
MONEY NOW IN GOD'S KINGDOM, WE WILL
RECEIVE GREAT REWARDS LATER IN
HEAVEN.**

Consider the implications of Christ's offer. We can
trade temporal possessions we can't keep to gain
eternal possessions we can't lose. This is like a child
trading bubble gum for a new bicycle, or a man
offered ownership of The Coca-Cola Company in
exchange for a sack of bottle caps. Only a fool would
pass up the opportunity.

What we keep we will lose. What we give and share
and do in Christ's name will ultimately come back to
us in heaven, in a far better and permanent form.

Whatever treasures we store up on earth will be left behind when we leave. Whatever treasures we store up in heaven will be waiting for us when we arrive.

The reality of eternal rewards inevitably fosters an investment mentality. For instance, with $15,000 I may be able to buy a new car. With the same money, I could help translate the Scriptures for an unreached people group, support church planting, feed the hungry in the name of Christ, get gospel literature distributed in Southeast Asia, or send out multiple Nigerian or Indian missionary families and support them full-time for a year. If I have an investment mentality, I ask myself, *What's the better investment for eternity?* If I need a car, I may ask, *Can I buy a used one and give away the difference to God's kingdom?*

A SAFE PLACE FOR YOUR MONEY?

Note that the central focus of Matthew 6:19-24 is not the renunciation of earthly treasures but the accumulation of heavenly treasures. We're to avoid storing up unnecessary treasures on earth not as an end in itself, but as a life strategy to lay up treasures in heaven. It's important to realize a person may give up all earthly treasures without ever investing in heavenly treasures. Our Lord is not looking for ascetics or hermits but eternity-wise investors.

Jesus is not speculating; he's speaking of certainties. When he warns us not to store up treasures on earth, it's not just because wealth *might* be lost. It's because wealth will *definitely* be lost. Either it leaves us while we live, or we leave it when we die. Treasures on earth are all flammable. The only way to fireproof them is to turn them into treasures in heaven.

A. W. Tozer said, "Any temporal possession can be turned into everlasting wealth. Whatever is given to Christ is immediately touched with immortality."[3]

Now that's something to get excited about!

"Naked a man comes from his mother's womb, and as he comes, so he departs. He takes nothing from his labor that he can carry in his hand" (Ecclesiastes 5:15).

You can't take it with you.

When Jesus speaks of moths and rust and thieves taking our earthly treasures, he is saying in effect: "You can't take it with you." But then he adds something breathtaking, something revolutionary, a brand-new corollary to the old adage: "You can't take it with you, but . . . *you can send it on ahead.*"

What a stunning qualification. My book *The Treasure Principle* centers on this concept. It's one of the keys to understanding and living the law of rewards. Who would have dared to think such a thing possible—that we creatures of dust could make choices today that would result in possessing eternal treasures in heaven? Jesus says, "Here's how you can do that: Take treasures you could have stored up on earth, only to eventually lose them, and instead store them up in heaven, where they'll remain intact forever."

People are always looking for safe places to put their money. Jesus says there's ultimately only one safe place: God's kingdom. By wisely and generously using our earthly resources, which means forgoing some earthly treasures, we can store up treasures in heaven.

Paul told the rich in this world that through their generosity and good deeds they may "lay up treasure for themselves as a firm foundation for the coming age" (1 Timothy 6:19). Christians throughout the ages have taken these passages literally. Consequently, they have been far less serious than we are about earthly treasures, and far more serious about heavenly treasures.

John Bunyan wrote *Pilgrim's Progress* from an English prison cell to which he had been condemned for unlicensed preaching of the gospel. This is how he interpreted the words of Christ and Paul:

> Whatever good thing you do for Him, if done according to the Word, is laid up for you as treasure in chests and coffers, to be brought out to be rewarded before both men and angels, to your eternal comfort.[4]

Is this a biblical concept? Absolutely. Paul spoke about the Philippians' financial giving and explained, "Not that I am looking for a gift, but I am looking for what may be credited to your account" (Philippians 4:17). God keeps an account open for us in heaven, and every gift given for his glory is a deposit in that account. Not only God, not only others, but *we* are the eternal beneficiaries of our giving.

Have you been making regular deposits into your account in heaven?

CHAPTER 3

GAINING WHAT YOU CAN'T LOSE

*He is no fool who gives what he cannot keep
to gain what he cannot lose.*
JIM ELLIOT

Although Christ's words in Matthew 6 can be applied in principle to investing the treasures of our time and talents, I believe the primary meaning involves releasing earthly money and possessions to obtain eternal treasures in heaven.

INEXHAUSTIBLE TREASURE

The first indicator that Jesus is talking about our money is the *context* of his remarks. He began this segment of the Sermon on the Mount by addressing the spiritual disciplines of giving, praying, and fasting. Because he had been talking about giving—making reference to putting money in the temple offering—his audience would naturally understand that the recommendation to "store up for yourselves treasures in heaven" is an elaboration on giving.

Second, the word *treasure* has a self-evident literal meaning. His listeners knew that "treasures on earth" were money, gems, gold, land, houses, livestock, and other valued possessions. When Jesus

WE PROVIDE TANGIBLE ASSETS FOR OURSELVES IN HEAVEN BY GIVING AWAY TANGIBLE ASSETS ON EARTH. told them not to store up their treasures on earth but in heaven, they would naturally conclude he was saying to draw the line at some point of material accumulation and give financially to purposes close to God's heart.

Third, the clincher is the parallel expression in Luke 12:33, where Jesus unmistakably connects giving with providing "treasure in heaven":

> Sell your possessions and give to the poor. Provide purses [some translations say *money belts*] for yourselves that will not wear out, a treasure in heaven that will not be exhausted, where no thief comes near and no moth destroys.

The use of *thief* and *moth* and *treasure*, and the injunction to provide money belts "for yourselves," shows that this passage in Luke is another way of saying the same thing as Matthew 6, though it was spoken a little differently on another occasion. This passage unmistakably links selling one's possessions with giving them away, and thereby producing treasures in heaven. The point is not asceticism, divesting ourselves of money because it's bad. Rather, the purpose is ministry, helping the poor and needy by giving them money because it's useful.

The picture of the "money belt" or "purse" that doesn't wear out further develops the concept of heavenly treasures. Our giving is the conduit or means that safely delivers the treasures to heaven. We provide tangible assets for ourselves in heaven by giving away, for the glory of God and the good of others, tangible assets on earth.

Jesus adds an insight in Luke 12 not present in Matthew 6. Not only is heavenly treasure not subject to thieves and moths, not only will the heavenly money belt not wear out, but there is "a treasure in heaven that will not be exhausted." This means not only that these heavenly treasures are safe and inde-structible, as Matthew 6 suggests, but that they are also *inexhaustible.* That is, they can be *used* in heaven without ever being *used up.*

In other words, someone who gives a child a drink of water out of kindness on earth will receive in heaven a reward that can be enjoyed without being consumed. On earth, someone might see his good deed and bake him a cake, which he would gratefully eat. But then it would be gone. In heaven we can enjoy and use our rewards, our heavenly treasures—whatever they may be—without ever exhausting them.

The law of rewards, which God has built into the universe, requires that every act of kindness and obedience be rewarded. But not only will there be rewards in heaven for the cup of water given on earth, those rewards *will never disappear.* The act of kind-ness will be remembered forever and its reward will always last. Hence, eternal rewards are not only rewards we'll receive in eternity, but rewards that are themselves eternal, imperishable, and inexhaustible (1 Peter 1:4).

REWARD PRINCIPLE #3: GOD OFFERS US REWARDS THAT ARE ETERNAL, IMPERISHABLE, AND INEXHAUSTIBLE.

Moses prayed in the oldest psalm, "Establish the work of our hands" (Psalm 90:17). The literal translation is "*Make permanent* the work of our hands." This is our heart's desire—that we would do things here and now that would survive this world, bearing fruit forever in the world to come. That is exactly what Christ promises us.

Do you believe him?

CONFEDERATE CURRENCY

John Wesley said, "Money never stays with me. It would burn me if it did. I throw it out of my hands as soon as possible, lest it should find its way into my heart."

Wesley earned considerable book royalties. At a time when a single man could live comfortably on thirty pounds a year, his annual income reached fourteen hundred.[5] Yet Wesley's goal was to give so generously that he would leave virtually nothing behind when he died. He achieved that goal.

What perspective motivated John Wesley to live this way? I use this analogy in my book *The Treasure Principle:*

Imagine you're alive at the end of the Civil War. You're living in the South, but you are a Northerner. You plan to

move home as soon as the war is over. While in the South you've accumulated lots of Confederate currency. Now, suppose you know for a fact that the North is going to win the war and the end is imminent. *What will you do with your Confederate money?*

If you're smart, there's only one answer. You should immediately cash in your Confederate currency for U.S. currency—the only money that will have value once the war is over. Keep only enough Confederate currency to meet your short-term needs.[6]

This is exactly why John Wesley lived as he did. When he left this world, he didn't want to be holding on to a pile of worthless Confederate money that he couldn't take with him.

When the Lord returns, all remaining money and possessions will burn, like wood, hay, and straw, when it could have been given in exchange for gold, silver, and precious stones. Money that could have been used to feed the hungry and fulfill the great commission will go up in smoke.

While it still had value, Wesley traded in his "Confederate currency" for treasures in heaven.

How about you and me? How much Confederate

money will we have left when we die or Christ returns?

Have you ever played one of those card games where the winner is the one who runs out of cards first? At the end of the game, every card left counts against you. The American dream is to die with as many cards in your hand as possible. But maybe we've got it backwards. Maybe our strategy should be like John Wesley's—not to get stuck with all those cards at our life's end.

"But the day of the Lord will come like a thief. The heavens will disappear with a roar; the elements will be destroyed by fire, and the earth and everything in it will be laid bare" (2 Peter 3:10).

We've been given an insider's knowledge of a coming change in the worldwide economic situation. The currency of this world will be worthless at our death or Christ's return, both of which are imminent. This knowledge should radically affect our invest-ment strategy. For us to accumulate vast earthly trea-sures in the face of the inevitable future is equivalent to stockpiling Confederate money. It's not just wrong. It's stupid.

Kingdom currency, backed by the eternal treasury, is the only medium of exchange recognized by the Son of God, whose government will last forever. The currency of his kingdom is our present faithful service and sacrificial use of our resources for him. The payoff in eternity will be what Paul called "a firm foundation," consisting of treasures beyond our wild-est dreams.

Are you stockpiling Confederate currency? Or are you exchanging it for kingdom currency that will survive this world . . . and retain its value for all eternity?

CHAPTER 4

TWO PERSPECTIVES, TWO MASTERS

He who has God and everything has no more than he who has God alone.

C. S. LEWIS

Suppose I offer you one thousand dollars to spend today however you want. Not a bad deal. But suppose I give you a choice. You can either have that thousand dollars today, or you can have ten million dollars if you'll wait one year—then ten million more every year thereafter.

What would you choose?

Only a fool would take the thousand dollars today. Yet that's what we do when we grab on to what will last for only a moment, forgoing something far more valuable we could enjoy later for much longer. A year may seem a long time to wait. But after it's done—as when our lives here are done—it will seem like it passed incredibly quickly. Early in that year, some may gloat about how they have the thousand dollars and we don't. But as the year goes on, every day their little treasure fades, while our huge treasure gets closer.

WHERE IS YOUR HEART?

Christ's words are profound: "Where your treasure is, there your heart will be also" (Matthew 6:21).

What we do with our possessions is a sure indicator of what's in our hearts. Jesus is saying, "Show me your checkbook, your credit card statement, and your receipts for cash expenditures, and I'll show you where your heart is." What we do with our money doesn't lie. It's a bold statement to God of what we truly value.

ASK GOD

✢ *You have entrusted me with many resources. Is that an indication you have given me the gift of giving and want me to learn to exercise it more frequently and skillfully?*

✢ *Where in the world (and in my community) do you want me to go, to see, and to participate in Christ-centered ministries meeting physical and spiritual needs?*

✢ *Am I treating you as owner and CEO of my assets, or am I treating you merely as a financial consultant to whom I pay a fee (10 percent or greater)?*

✢ *Am I living to hear others say of me, "He's a great success" or to have you say to me, "Well done, my good and faithful servant"?*

But what we do with our money doesn't simply *indicate* where our heart *is*. According to Jesus, it *determines* where our heart *goes*. This is an amazing and exciting truth. If I want my heart to be in one particular place and not in another, then I need to put my money in that place and not in the other.

I've heard people say, "I want more of a heart for missions." I always respond, "Jesus tells you exactly how to get it. Put your money in missions, and your heart will follow."

Do you wish you had a greater heart for the poor and lost? Then give your money to help the poor and reach the lost. Do you want your heart to be in your church? Put your money there. Your heart will always be where your money is. Your heart will never be where your money isn't. If most of your money is in mutual funds, retirement, your house, or your hobby, that's where your heart is going to be.

That doesn't mean it is wrong to have some money in earthly things. Nor does it mean that earthly things can't be used as they are—without liquidating them—to serve God's purposes.

"In the house of the wise are stores of choice food and oil, but a foolish man devours all he has" (Proverbs 21:20). The ant is commended because "it stores its provisions in summer and gathers its food at harvest" (Proverbs 6:6-8). It's a shortsighted person who fails to store up provisions (money, food, or materials) for upcoming times of predictable need.

Yet there's a point where accumulating money and possessions becomes stockpiling, which generates a strong gravitational hold on our hearts. Saving becomes hoarding when it's asserting our financial independence so we imagine we don't have to trust

God anymore. Retirement savings and insurance can be excessive and too easily become our source of security, turning into idols.

Giving is the alternative to spending or hoarding that breaks the back of materialism. The act of giving is a vivid reminder that it's all about God, not about us. Giving is a joyful surrender to a greater person and a greater agenda. It affirms Christ's lordship. Giving dethrones me and exalts him. It breaks the chains of mammon that would enslave me. It makes heaven, not earth, my center of gravity.

"My heart isn't in the things of God." Is it because your treasure isn't in the things of God? Put your resources, your assets, your money and possessions, your time and talents and energies into the things of God. As surely as the compass needle follows north, your heart will follow your treasure.

Money leads; hearts follow.

TWO PERSPECTIVES

After discussing the two treasures, Jesus speaks of two perspectives: "The eye is the lamp of the body. If your eyes are good, your whole body will be full of light. But if your eyes are bad, your whole body will be full of darkness" (Matthew 6:22-23). Jesus makes it clear that our vision is faulty. We need his help to see our life through different eyes—eyes focused on the eternal.

Physical vision is used here as a metaphor for spiritual vision, or *perspective*—the way we look at life. Unbelievers view life as a brief interval that begins at birth and ends at death. In considering the future, they look no further than their own life span, if even that. Their vision is pitifully short and narrow, restricted to the horizons of this world. Like a myopic horse with blinders on, the person without Christ can see neither far nor wide.

Bereft of eternal perspective, unbelievers are bound to take wrong turns and come to wrong conclusions, thinking, *If this life is all there is, why deny myself any pleasure or possession?* Given this premise, why would they come to any other conclusion? People only *live* for a higher purpose when they *see* a higher purpose.

As believers in Christ, our theology gives us perspective. It tells us that this life is the preface—not the book. It's the preliminaries—not the main event. It's the tune-up—not the concert.

When you're on a long airplane flight, you naturally socialize, eat, read, pray, sleep, and maybe talk about where you're going. But what would you think if a passenger in the window seat hung curtains over the window, taped photographs to the seat in front of him, and put up wall hangings? You'd think, *Hey, it's not that long of a trip. Once we get to the destination, none of this will matter.*

I think of our lives in terms of a dot and a line, signifying two phases. Our present life on earth is the dot. It begins. It ends. It's brief. However, from the dot, a line extends that goes on forever. That line is eternity, which Christians will spend in heaven.

Right now we're living *in* the dot. But what are we living *for?* The shortsighted person lives for the dot. The person with perspective lives for the line.

Like evangelism and Bible study and moral purity, giving is living for the line.

It's all about perspective. The believer's view of reality should be radically different than the non-believer's. We should live differently because we see differently. We witness the same current events but interpret them differently. We eat the same food and exchange the same currency but live according to two different purposes. These purposes are based squarely on two different perspectives—one that looks at life in the short run and the other that looks at life in the long run.

When our eyes are set on eternity, the news that someone has come to know the Savior means a great deal more than the news of a salary raise or the prospect of getting the latest high-tech gadget. Of course, the salary raise, and perhaps the gadget, can be used for the kingdom of God. But the point is that neither one in itself is ultimately important, whereas new birth, which affects the eternal destiny of a precious human being, is vitally important. So important that the inhabitants of heaven rejoice over it the moment it happens (Luke 15:7, 10).

The one with good eyes, the one with an eternal perspective, is accurate in his appraisal of what's important. With vision corrected by God's Word, this person sees life through the eyes of eternity.

Unlike others, the believer stares through the haze and peers beyond the horizons of this world to another.

MOMENTARY SACRIFICE, ETERNAL GAIN

The patriarchs lived as "aliens and strangers on earth," spending their days "longing for a better country—a heavenly one" (Hebrews 11:13-16). Peter encouraged Christians to find joy by focusing not on the trial that will go on only "a little while," but on their heavenly inheritance that will never perish (1 Peter 1:4-9). Paul said, "I consider that our present sufferings are not worth comparing with the glory that will be revealed in us" (Romans 8:18). "For our light and momentary troubles are achieving for us an eternal glory that far outweighs them all" (2 Corinthians 4:17).

Paul speaks not of a glory achieved for Christ but "for us." Likewise, Jesus didn't say, "Store up for *me* treasures in heaven"; he said, "Store up *for yourselves* treasures in heaven" (Matthew 6:20, italics mine). Of course, only Christ will be honored as the object of our worship in heaven. We will gladly lay our crowns, our rewards, before his throne, so he receives the ultimate glory (Revelation 4:10-11). Yet Scripture teaches that we will not only behold his glory but participate in it (Romans 8:18-19).

Paul spoke about the Philippians' financial giving, explaining, "Not that I am looking for a gift, but I am looking for what may be credited to your account" (Philippians 4:17). God keeps an account open for us in heaven, and every gift given for his glory is a deposit in that account.

When we give, we withdraw funds from our earthly account to have them credited to our heavenly account. Not only God, not only others, but we are the eternal beneficiaries of our giving.

The money God entrusts to us is eternal investment capital. Every day is an opportunity to buy up more shares in his kingdom.

You can't take it with you, but you can send it on ahead.

It's a revolutionary concept that changed my life and my family's. If you embrace it, I guarantee it will change your life too.

THE MOST HIGH YIELDS

Financial planners have a hard time convincing people to look ahead instead of focusing on today, this week, or this year. "Don't think just one year ahead," they'll tell you. "Think thirty years ahead." But the truth is, thinking thirty years ahead is only slightly less shortsighted than thinking thirty days ahead. Wise people think ahead not just to the retirement years, not merely to the end of their earthly life, but to *eternity*. We shouldn't say, "Think thirty years ahead," but "Think thirty *million* years ahead."

Financial counselors point out the difference between investing the same yearly amounts in an individual retirement account starting at age twenty-five or age forty. At retirement, the bottom-line difference is huge. This is good insight for the Christian who is storing up for eternity: The sooner you get started, the more you'll have await-ing you.

A financial counselor will say, "You can't go back at age sixty-five and snap your fingers to compen-sate for forty years of poor planning." But what's far more important is that you can't reach the end of your life, snap your fingers, and compensate for a lifetime of poor planning to meet God. The rich fool is proof of that.

God's eternal prospectus bears a careful look in light of its guaranteed rate of interest. Jesus prom-ises an ultimate return of a hundred times—a 10,000 percent rate of interest that lasts forever (Matthew 19:29). What earthly investment compares to that?

Based on Christ's words, let me assume the role of "eternal financial counselor" and offer some advice: *Choose your investments carefully, compare rates of interest, and evaluate how your investments will be working for you a few million years from now.*

Unbelievers see with what Jesus called the "bad eye." The Christian's view of finances, seen through a "good eye," should be radically different. True, we may participate in some of the same earthly invest-ments. Occasionally our short-term goals will appear similar. But our long-term goals and purposes should be fundamentally different.

TWO MASTERS

Having already spoken of two treasuries and two perspectives, Jesus now speaks of two masters. He says that although we might *have* both God and money, we cannot *serve* both God and money.

I might have two jobs, three sisters, or five friends, but only one spouse. Some relationships by their nature are exclusive. The most basic of these is our relationship with God. There's a throne in each life only big enough for one. Christ may occupy that throne. Money may occupy that throne. But both cannot occupy that throne.

Christ's words raise three questions—Are you investing in the right treasury? Are you adopting the right perspective? Are you serving the right master?

There's nothing wrong with having money. We need it to live on while we're still living in this foreign land. God graciously provides it for us. But we must understand its limits. Like Confederate money near the end of the Civil War, it's only good for a very short period of time, and that time is running out. It will be worthless once we get home. We're here on earth on a short-term visa. One day soon it's going to expire.

Jesus gave us a choice—a life wasted in the pursuit of wealth on earth, or a life invested in the pursuit of wealth in heaven. Every heartbeat brings us one moment closer to eternity.

Every day, the person whose treasure is on earth is headed *away* from his treasure. Every day, the person whose treasure is in heaven is headed *toward* his treasure. Whoever spends his life heading away from his treasure has reason to despair. Whoever spends his life headed toward his treasure has reason to rejoice.

Where's your treasure? Are you heading toward it or away from it? Do you have reason to despair or reason to rejoice?

John Wesley made his choice. Have you made yours?

Is it time to start relocating your treasure?

CHAPTER 5

LOOKING THROUGH ETERNITY'S LENS

*It ought to be the business of every day
to prepare for our last day.*
MATTHEW HENRY

An ancient story goes like this: A slave travels with his master to Baghdad. Early one morning, while milling through the marketplace, the slave sees death in human form. Death gives him a threatening look. The slave recoils in terror, convinced that Death intends to take him that day.

The slave runs to his master and says, "Help me. I have seen Death, and the look in his eyes tells me he intends to take my life this very day. Please, master, let me leave now and flee on camel so that by tonight I can reach Samara, where Death will not find me."

His master agrees, and the terrified servant rides like the wind for the fifteen-hour journey to Samara.

A few hours later, the master sees Death among the throngs in Baghdad. He boldly approaches Death and asks him, "Why did you give my servant a threatening look?"

"That was not a threatening look," Death replies. "That was a look of surprise. You see, I was amazed to

THE SINGLE
GREATEST
CONTRIBUTOR TO
OUR INABILITY TO
SEE MONEY AND
POSSESSIONS IN
THEIR TRUE LIGHT
IS OUR PERSIS-
TENT FAILURE TO
SEE OUR PRESENT
LIVES THROUGH
THE LENS OF
ETERNITY.

see your servant today in Baghdad, for I have an appointment with him tonight in Samara."

True, the story's imagery is misleading—it's our righteous Master, not Death, who has the power to call us home at his appointed time. But the moral is on target. The time of our death is unknown. The way of our death is unpredictable. But the fact of our death is inescapable. The statistics are unwavering: 100 percent of those who are born die. We may spend our lives running from death and denying death, but that won't stop death from coming at its appointed time. "No man has power over the wind to contain it; so no one has power over the day of his death" (Ecclesiastes 8:8).

Talking about death won't bring it a moment sooner. But it will give us opportunity to prepare for what lies ahead. If life's greatest certainty is death, wouldn't it be foolish not to prepare for what lies beyond this life? Any life that leaves us unprepared for death is a wasted life.

What does this have to do with money and possessions, or the law of rewards? It has *everything* to do with it. The single greatest contributor to our inability to see money and possessions in their true light—and our tendency to ignore the law of rewards—is our persistent failure to see our present lives through the lens of eternity.

> **REWARD PRINCIPLE #4: WHEN WE SEE OUR LIVES THROUGH THE LENS OF ETERNITY, OUR ATTITUDE TOWARD WEALTH WILL CHANGE DRASTICALLY.**

THE LOST SENSE OF THE ETERNAL

A startling thing has happened among Western Christians. Many of us habitually think and act as if there were no eternity—or as if what we do in this present life has no eternal consequences.

How many sermons about heaven or hell have most of us heard lately? How many modern gospel booklets even mention the words *heaven* or *hell?* The trend is to focus on our present circumstances instead of our eternal future. Yet Scripture states that eternal realities should influence the character of our present life, right down to every word we speak and every action we take (James 2:12; 2 Peter 3:11-12).

In those rare times when we do seriously consider the afterlife, it seems strange or dreamlike, so otherworldly as to be unreal.

As I say in my book *In Light of Eternity,* Satan deceives us into thinking of the afterlife as a ghostlike existence, while Scripture portrays it in very tangible and earthy ways. He deceives us in order to turn our minds away from the wonders of heaven, our true home, and set them on things that will not matter in eternity.[7]

So we come back to "reality"—our present lives

and possessions that we can see, hear, touch, feel, and taste. Things are real. *Now* is real. We return to the pressing business of the day, that which is immediately relevant, those all-important matters of the present. These might include what's happening in Hollywood, on Wall Street, in Washington or London, or in the NFL or NBA; or what new self-help technique can make us beautiful or happy; or how we can decorate our house; or what kind of car we want to buy; or where we can get a low-interest loan. We live as if these shadowlands were the real world, the ultimate reality. But Scripture tells us they are not.

GOD'S WORDS AS A GUIDE

"For we will all stand before God's judgment seat. . . . Each of us will give an account of himself to God." (Romans 14:10, 12)

"From everyone who has been given much, much will be demanded; and from the one who has been entrusted with much, much more will be asked." (Luke 12:48)

The Bible tells us we are pilgrims, strangers, aliens, ambassadors working far from home (Hebrews 11:13; 2 Corinthians 5:20). Our citizenship is in heaven (Philippians 3:20). But we've become so attached to this world that we live for the wrong kingdom. We forget our true home, built for us by our bridegroom

(John 14:1-2). Paul said, "I desire to depart and be with Christ, which is better by far" (Philippians 1:23).

C. S. Lewis said, "Our Father refreshes us on the journey with some pleasant inns, but will not encourage us to mistake them for home."[8] Too many of us spend our lives mistaking these temporary residences for our true home. But our home is in another place— and each day we are one day closer to it.

God says this life is so brief that we are like grass that grows up in the morning and wilts in the afternoon (Isaiah 40:6-8). Our existence here is but "mist that appears for a little while and then vanishes" (James 4:14).

When my friend Leona Bryant discovered she had only a short time to live, she told me of radical changes in her perspective. "The most striking thing that's happened," she said, "is that I find myself totally uninterested in all the conversations about material things. Things used to matter to me, but now I find my thoughts are never on possessions, but always on Christ and people. I consider it a privilege that I can live each day, knowing I will die soon. What a difference it makes!"

Recently another dying friend told me with a smile, "I don't buy jumbo shampoo like I used to. I don't even buy green bananas." She knew where she was going. And she knew she wouldn't be here much longer. Neither will we.

David prayed,

> Show me, O Lord, my life's end and the number of my days; let me know how fleeting is my life.

OUR CITIZENSHIP
IS IN HEAVEN, BUT
WE'VE BECOME SO
ATTACHED TO THIS
WORLD THAT WE
LIVE FOR THE
WRONG KINGDOM.

You have made my days a mere handbreadth; the span of my years is as notl.ing before you. Each man's life is but a breath. Man is a mere phantom as he goes to and fro: He bustles about, but only in vain; he heaps up wealth, not knowing who will get it. But now, Lord, what do I look for? My hope is in you. (Psalm 39:4-7)

Because this life is so brief, we might conclude it's inconsequential. Our lives may seem like pebbles dropped in a pond. They create ripples for a moment, tiny wrinkles that smooth out, then are gone forever. Abandoned tombstones with names no one remembers are stark reminders of our eventual anonymity in this world. What do you know about your great-grandparents? What will your great-grandchildren know about you?

Our brief stay here may appear unimportant, but nothing could be further from the truth. The Bible tells us that although others may not remember us or care what our lives here have been, God will remember perfectly, and he cares very much—so much that the door of eternity swings on the hinges of our present lives.

The Bible tells us that this life lays the foundation upon which eternal life is built. Eternity will hold for us what we have invested there during our life on earth.

Scripture makes clear that the one central business of this life is to prepare for the next.

THE LONG TOMORROW: WHAT LIES AHEAD?

As no piece of a puzzle can be understood apart from the greater context of the full puzzle, so our present lives—including what we should do with all our money and possessions—cannot be understood apart from the greater context of eternity. In the rest of the chapter, I'll try to paint the backdrop of what A. W. Tozer called "the long tomorrow," against which the question of money—and all questions of life—must be properly viewed.

DEATH AND JUDGMENT

The old saying "Nothing is certain but death and taxes" is half true. There are tax evaders, but there are no death evaders. Those alive at the return of Christ may not technically die, but the result will be the same—their earthly lives will end abruptly, and they will move immediately to the afterlife.

Hebrews 9:27 explains our written-in-stone itinerary: "Man is destined to die once, and after that to face judgment." This judgment is for all people, not some. Whether we go to Christ in death or he comes to us in his return, we face judgment.

There is built into every person, society, and religion a basic belief that good deserves reward and evil deserves punishment, and both will ultimately get what they deserve. God has written his moral law on human hearts (Romans 2:12-16). This includes an inborn sense that one day we will be judged by that law.

Scripture confirms this inbred expectation of judgment. It says that God will judge everyone (Acts 17:31), and he will judge fairly (Genesis

18:25). Specifically, he will judge us according to our deeds: "I the Lord search the heart and examine the mind, to reward a man according to his conduct, according to what his deeds deserve" (Jeremiah 17:10).

All people should live each day with this awesome awareness: "But they will have to give account to him who is ready to judge the living and the dead" (1 Peter 4:5).

His judgment extends to what is hidden to others: "God will bring every deed into judgment, including every hidden thing, whether it is good or evil" (Ecclesiastes 12:14). He knows the motives of men's hearts and judges us accordingly (1 Corinthians 4:5).

We are all sinners, and the wages of sin is death (Romans 3:23; 6:23). But a holy God, out of love for us, judged Jesus for our sins (Isaiah 53:9-10). Only by embracing Christ's atonement for our sins can we escape the everlasting punishment due us (Romans 6:23; 2 Corinthians 5:21). God's justice was satisfied, but only at the cost of his own blood. To purchase our redemption, Jesus experienced an eternity of hell in a few hours on the cross.

Dietrich Bonhoeffer was right: grace is free, but it is not cheap. Jesus' sacrifice writes our name in the Lamb's Book of Life, saving believers from the judgment that leads to hell. However—and this is something rarely proclaimed in most churches—we will face another judgment for our actions on earth. We'll talk about that in the next chapter.

THE UNBELIEVER'S JUDGMENT IN HELL

Hell is a place of punishment designed for Satan and the fallen angels (Matthew 25:41-46; Revelation 20:10). However, it will also be inhabited by those who do not accept God's gift of redemption in Christ (Revelation 20:12-15).

Hell is an actual place, clearly and graphically spoken of by Jesus (Matthew 10:28; 13:40-42; Mark 9:43-44). Hell is indescribably dreadful. If we trust the Bible, we must realize that hell is undeniably real. Hell is something most of us do not want to believe in. But who are we to tell God he's wrong? He so wants us not to go to hell that he paid the ultimate price so we wouldn't have to. Nevertheless, apart from trusting Christ for salvation, any person's eternal future will be spent in hell.

Because God is fair, hell won't be the same for everyone. The severity of punishment will vary with the degree of truth known and the nature and number of sins committed. This concept is foreign to most Christians, but it is clearly taught in Scripture (Matthew 11:20-24; Luke 20:45-47; Romans 2:3-5). This is no consolation, however, since the "best" of hell will still be hell—eternal exclusion from the presence of God and the soothing light of his grace.

THE BELIEVER'S EXPERIENCE IN HEAVEN

Jesus commands us to store up for ourselves treasures in heaven. Yet because we've bought into misconceptions of heaven, failing to look at what Scripture tells us, we cling to earth as our home. Naturally, then, we tend to lay up our treasures here rather than there. Because we cannot devote our lives to laying up treasures in a heaven we're not looking forward to, it's critical that we take time here to address the question of what heaven is like.

At this point some people always object that they don't want to be the kind of person who is "so heavenly minded they are of no earthly good." While I've often heard that expression, I've never once met someone of whom it was true! In fact, we are *commanded* to "set your minds on things above, not on earthly things" (Colossians 3:2). Our problem isn't that we're too heavenly minded but that we're too earthly minded. That's exactly why Jesus commanded us to stop storing up treasures on earth and start storing them up in heaven. A. W. Tozer said,

> It has been cited as a flaw in Christianity that it is more concerned with the world to come than with the world that now is. . . . No one who knows what the New Testament is about will worry over the charge that Christianity is other-worldly. Of course it is, and that is precisely where its power lies.[9]

CHAPTER 6

HEAVEN: THE HOME WE'VE NEVER BEEN

Hearts on earth say in the course of a joyful experience, "I don't want this ever to end." But it invariably does. The hearts of those in heaven say, "I want this to go on forever." And it will. There can be no better news than this.

J. I. PACKER

As he was about to leave this world, Jesus said to his disciples, "There are many rooms in my Father's home, and I am going to prepare a place for you. . . . When everything is ready, I will come and get you, so that you will always be with me where I am" (John 14:2-3, NLT).

We were made for a person and a place. Jesus is the person. Heaven is the place.

Jesus is the one preparing that place for us. And he's also preparing us for that place.

A good carpenter envisions what he wants to build. He plans and designs. Then he does his work, carefully and skillfully fashioning it to exact specifications. He takes pride in the work he's done and loves to show it off. And Jesus isn't just any carpenter—we already know he's the creator of the world and he built everything we see. Heaven is his greatest building project.

For Christians, heaven is our home. Paul said, "[We] would prefer to be away from the body and at home with the Lord" (2 Corinthians 5:8). Home is the place of acceptance, security, rest, refuge, deep personal relationships, and great memories.

WHAT WILL HEAVEN BE LIKE?

God's people, aliens and strangers on earth, spend their lives "looking forward to a country they can call their own" and "looking for a better place, a heavenly homeland" (Hebrews 11:14, 16, NLT). The capital of this heavenly country will be a "city with eternal foundations, a city designed and built by God" (Hebrews 11:10, NLT). This city will have all the freshness, vitality, and openness of the country with all the vibrancy, interdependence, and relationships of a city—one without crime, litter, smog, sirens, seaminess, or slums.

Christ promised we would eat and drink with him—along with Abraham and Isaac and Jacob and a host of others (Matthew 8:11). We'll meet and converse with other inhabitants of heaven. Not only Abraham, but Moses, David, Ruth, Esther, Mary, and Peter. I look forward to conversations with C. S. Lewis, A. W. Tozer, Jonathan Edwards, Charles Spurgeon, and Amy Carmichael.

God will surely not give us less creativity in heaven but *more,* unmarred by sin, unlimited by mortality. We will compose, write, paint, carve, build, plant, and grow.

There will be no temple, no church buildings. Christ will be the focus of all. Worship will be unaffected, without pretense or distraction. We'll be lost in our worship, overcome by God's magnificence and the privilege of being his children.

Heaven will offer much-needed rest to the weary (Revelation 14:13). What feels better than putting your head on the pillow after a hard day's work or kicking back to read a good book with a cold drink by your side? But rest renews us, revitalizes us to become active again. Heaven will offer refreshing activity, productive and unthwarted—like Adam and Eve's work in Eden before sin brought the curse on the ground.

In heaven, we're told, "his servants will serve him" (Revelation 22:3). This means we'll be active, because to "serve" means to work, to expend effort, to do something. Service involves responsibilities, duties, effort, planning, and creativity to do work well. Those who speak of heaven in terms of rest are only seeing part of the picture. It's not just a place of rest but one of enriching activity and lasting accomplishments.

We'll lead and exercise authority in heaven, making important decisions. We'll reign with Christ (2 Timothy 2:12; Revelation 3:21), not temporarily but "for ever and ever" (Revelation 22:5). "Reigning" implies specific delegated responsibilities for those under our leadership (Luke 19:17-19). We'll rule over the world and even over angels (1 Corinthians 6:2-3).

When God brings heaven down to the new earth, he "will wipe every tear from their eyes" (Revelation 21:4). What an intimate picture—God's hands will touch the face of each individual child, removing

HEAVEN IS THE
CHRISTIAN'S
CERTAIN HOPE,
A HOPE THAT
CAN AND SHOULD
SUSTAIN US
THROUGH LIFE'S
DARKEST HOURS.

every tear. The same verse says, "There will be no more death or mourning or crying or pain." As the Irish poet Thomas Moore put it, "Earth has no sorrow that Heaven cannot heal."

No hospitals. No cemeteries. No sin. No evil. No fear. No abuse, rape, murder, drugs, drunkenness, bombs, guns, or terrorism.

God is the creator of diversity. People of every tribe and nation and tongue will worship the Lamb together (Revelation 7:9-10). And on the new earth, capital planet of the new universe, leaders of nations will carry into the New Jerusalem cultural treasures that will bring glory to their creator (Revelation 21:24, 26).

Heaven will be the home of relentless joy. The greatest joy will be marrying and living with our bridegroom, Jesus Christ. If we love Christ, we long to be with him. The next greatest joy will be reuniting with our departed loved ones. I don't like to be away from my family, but what keeps me going is the anticipation of reunion. The longer the separation, the sweeter the reunion. Some Christians will be reunited with parents they've not seen for fifty years and with children lost long ago. For Christians, death is never the end of a relationship but only an interruption to be followed by glorious reunion (1 Thessalonians 4:13-18).

Heaven is the Christian's certain hope, a hope that

can and should sustain us through life's darkest hours. But this doesn't happen automatically. We must choose to think about heaven and center our lives around it: "Set your sights on the realities of heaven, where Christ sits at God's right hand. . . . Let heaven fill your thoughts" (Colossians 3:1-2, NLT).

When heaven fills our thoughts, we will never look at earthly money and possessions the same way. We will view them as kingdom capital—perishable instruments that can be used here and now to make an eternal difference in the home world, where we'll live forever.

THE COMING JUDGMENT

Scripture tells us there's a coming judgment of believers that will determine for all eternity our positions or roles in heaven.

The Bible teaches two eternal judgments, one for unbelievers and one for believers (John 5:28-29). All true believers will pass the judgment of faith in Christ. All unbelievers will fail the judgment of their faith in Christ at the great white throne, since their names are not written in the Book of Life (Revelation 20:11-15).

But faith is not the only thing judged. Scripture repeatedly states that all men, not just unbelievers, will be judged for their works (Proverbs 24:12; Ecclesiastes 12:14).

The believer will not be condemned at the great white throne, but nonetheless he or she still faces a judgment of works at what is called the "judgment seat of Christ."

THE BELIEVER'S JUDGMENT IN HEAVEN

The Lord's evaluation of the seven churches in Revelation 2 and 3 shows that he's watching us, evaluating us. He is "keeping score." As an instructor gives grades to his students, Christ gives grades to his churches. To Christians, Jesus says, "I am he who searches hearts and minds, and I will repay each of you according to your deeds" (Revelation 2:23).

Scripture teaches with unmistakable clarity that all believers in Christ will give an account of their lives to their Lord (Romans 14:10-12). We will be judged by him according to our works, both good and bad (2 Corinthians 5:10). The result of this will be the gain or loss of eternal rewards (1 Corinthians 3:12-15).

THIS, AGAIN, IS THE LAW
OF REWARDS: WHILE OUR
FAITH DETERMINES OUR
ETERNAL DESTINATION,
OUR BEHAVIOR DETERMINES
OUR ETERNAL REWARDS.

God's Word treats the judgment of believers with great sobriety. It does not portray it as a meaningless formality, going through the motions before we get on to the real business of heavenly bliss. Rather, Scripture presents it as a monumental event in which things of eternal significance are brought to light and things of eternal consequence are put into effect.

If any man builds on this foundation [Christ]
using gold, silver, costly stones, wood, hay or
straw, his work will be shown for what it is,
because the Day will bring it to light. It will be
revealed with fire, and the fire will test the quality of each man's work. If what he has built
survives, he will receive his reward. If it is
burned up, he will suffer loss; he himself will be
saved, but only as one escaping through the
flames. (1 Corinthians 3:12-15)

Our works are what we have done with our
resources—time, energy, talents, money, possessions.
The fire of God's holiness will reveal the quality of these
works, the eternal significance of what we've done with
our God-given assets and opportunities. The fate of the
works will be determined by their nature. If they are
made of the right stuff (gold, silver, costly stones), they'll
withstand and be purified by the fire. But no matter how
nice our works of wood, hay, and straw may look in the
display case of this world, they will not withstand the
incendiary gaze of God's Son in the next.

"We must all appear before the judgment seat of
Christ, that each one may receive what is due him for
the things done while in the body, whether good or
bad" (2 Corinthians 5:10).

"Whether good or bad" in the above verse may be
the most disturbing phrase in the New Testament. It's
so upsetting to hearers, in fact, that I've found any
honest attempts to deal with it are met with tremendous resistance.

When teaching at a Bible college, I read the words of this verse, without saying I was quoting Scripture. Then I asked, "How many of you agree with what I just said?" Only a few hands out of a hundred went up. This verse rubs against the grain of our thinking. But either God is wrong or we are! When we take the words at face value we say to ourselves, "But we *can't* experience recompense for bad things we've done—that contradicts grace and forgiveness."

Equally disturbing is the direct statement to Christians that not only will they receive reward from Christ for their good works, but "anyone who does wrong will be repaid for his wrong, and there is no favoritism" (Colossians 3:25). Since Christ has paid the price for our sins, if we have confessed and received forgiveness of our sins, what can this mean?

We must resist the temptation to immediately explain away such verses, instead of letting their weight fall upon us.

Our sins *are* totally forgiven when we come to Christ, and we *do* stand justified in him (Romans 5:1; 8:1). Scripture is emphatic on this point, and I am too. Nevertheless, the Bible speaks about a coming judgment of our works, not our sins. When we commit sins or neglect doing righteous acts we should have done, we are not doing what we could to lay up precious stones on the foundation of Christ. Therefore, these sins contribute to our "suffering loss." Through this loss of reward, the believer is considered to be receiving his "due" for his works, "whether good or bad." So what we do as believers, both good and bad, will have certain eternal effects.

"Let us throw off everything that hinders and the sin that so easily entangles, and let us run with perseverance the race marked out for us" (Hebrews 12:1). Sin entangles our feet, puts us out of the competition, and results in losing the race and the prize.

If we are his children, God is for us, not against us (Romans 8:31). He has assured us our names are written in the Book of Life, and we won't face the Great White Throne Judgment. He wants to commend and reward us at the judgment seat of Christ. He doesn't want the works of our lifetime to go up in smoke. He wants us to have eternal rewards—and he has given us every resource in Christ to live the godly life that will result in those eternal rewards (2 Peter 1:3).

FIVE MINUTES AFTER WE DIE

Five minutes after we die every Christian will understand that heaven is our home and earth was simply a temporary lodging on the homeward journey. Then we'll know for certain what was important and what wasn't. We will see with eternity's clarity. We will know exactly how we should have lived.

But we don't have to wait until we die to know how we should live. God has given us his Word to tell us how to live and his indwelling Spirit to empower us to live as we should.

We can either take off the blinders now, while we

still have our earthly lives to live, or wait for them to be taken off after death—when it will be too late to go back and change what we've done on earth.

May what will be most important to us five minutes after we die become most important to us now.

CHAPTER 7

DAILY SHAPING OUR ETERNAL FUTURE

He who provides for this life but takes not care for eternity is wise for a moment but a fool forever.
JOHN TILLOTSON

God calls us to obey him not simply because it's right but because it's smart. He warns us against disobedience not just because it's wrong but also because it's stupid. Hence, a man is told not to commit adultery because if he does he will not go unpunished (Proverbs 6:29). The appeal is not just to his spirituality but also to his common sense. Consider Christ's words in Matthew 7:24-26:

> Therefore everyone who hears these words of mine and puts them into practice is like a wise man who built his house on the rock. The rain came down, the streams rose, and the winds blew and beat against that house; yet it did not fall, because it had its foundation on the rock. But everyone who hears these words of mine and does not put them into practice is like a foolish man who built his house on sand. The rain came down, the streams rose, and the winds blew and beat against that house, and it fell with a great crash.

Notice that obedience is measured here not by its virtue but by its wisdom. Disobedience is measured not by its evil but by its fool-ishness. The man who obeys is not called a righteous man but a "wise man." The point is not that he is *virtuous* to follow God's commandments but that he is *smart* to do so. The one who disobeys is not called an evil man but a "foolish man." Why? Because rather than choosing the self-benefiting rewards of wisdom, he has chosen the self-punishing consequences of foolishness.

That's what Jesus was emphasizing in Matthew 6 when he commanded us to store up treasures for ourselves in heaven, where they will last, instead of on earth, where they'll be lost. He encouraged us to be smart, not stupid.

REWARD PRINCIPLE #5: OBEYING GOD IS NOT ONLY RIGHT, IT'S SMART. IT WILL ALWAYS PAY OFF IN THE END.

Remember Jim Elliot's famous statement we looked at earlier? We could paraphrase it another way: "He is a great fool who tries to hold on to what he cannot keep, only to lose what he could have gained."

That's exactly how most people spend their lives. How about you?

Disobeying God isn't just wrong . . . it's foolish.

Following Christ wholeheartedly isn't just right . . . it's wise.

Every time Scripture talks about the judgment seat of Christ, it is affirming this principle: Ultimately, when we stand before God, everything that is right will pay off enormously, and everything that is wrong will be seen to have been terribly stupid.

WHAT GOOD ARE WORKS?

For those who have served Christ faithfully, the judgment seat will be a time of commendation and celebration. He will reward us for acts of love that no one else even noticed.

The five-hundred-year-old play *Everyman* is a picture of all people. As Everyman faces Death, he looks among his friends for a companion. Only one friend would accompany him on the journey through death to final judgment. His name? "Good Deeds."

Some balk at such a picture. Yet it's explicitly biblical: "Then I heard a voice from heaven say, 'Write: Blessed are the dead who die in the Lord from now on.' 'Yes,' says the Spirit, 'they will rest from their labor, for their deeds will follow them'" (Revelation 14:13).

In Revelation 19:7-8, we're told "'The wedding of the Lamb has come, and his bride has made herself ready. Fine linen, bright and clean, was given her to wear.' (Fine linen stands for the righteous acts of the saints.)"

Note that the parenthetical statement in the preceding verse is not mine but God's. I once cited this verse in another book and the editor promptly "corrected" it, assuming it was my own interpretation. Why? Because it didn't sound right. But it is—it's Scripture!

We might expect to be told that *Christ* makes the bride ready, rather than she herself. We might expect that the fine linen would stand for "the righteousness of Christ," or perhaps "the righteous faith of the saints." But what we are told is that it stands for "the righteous *acts* of the saints."

We've been deceived into thinking that *works* is a dirty word. God condemns works done to earn salvation and works done to impress others. But our Lord enthusiastically *commends* works done for the right reasons. Immediately after saying our salvation is "not by works," Paul adds: "For we are God's workmanship, created in Christ Jesus to do good works, which God prepared in advance for us to do" (Ephesians 2:10). The fact that we frequently quote the previous verses and not verse 10 demonstrates our imbalance.

God has a lifetime of good works for each of us to do, including many works with our money and possessions. He will reward us according to whether or not we do them.

Scripture ties God's reward-giving to his character: "God is not unjust; he will not forget your work and the love you have shown him as you have helped his people and continue to help them" (Hebrews 6:10). The verses that follow in Hebrews 6 tell us that if we are to inherit God's promised blessings, we must not become lazy but be diligent in our God-given works.

The Law of Rewards

James repeatedly states that good works are essen-tial to the Christian life (James 2:17-18, 22, 24, 26). "Who is wise and understanding among you? Let him show it by his good life, by deeds done in the humility that comes from wisdom" (James 3:13).

GOD'S WORDS AS A GUIDE

"One thing God has spoken, two things have I heard: that you, O God, are strong, and that you, O Lord, are loving. Surely you will reward each person according to what he has done." (Psalm 62:11-12)

"Remember this: Whoever sows sparingly will also reap sparingly, and whoever sows generously will also reap generously. Each man should give what he has decided in his heart to give, not reluctantly or under compulsion, for God loves a cheerful giver." (2 Corinthians 9:6-7)

We know Christ will say to some (but not all) believers, "Well done, good and faithful servant!" (Matthew 25:21). Not "Well *said*" or "Well *believe*" but "Well *done*." What separates the sheep from goats is what they did and didn't do with their G entrusted resources of time, money, and posses

Peter says, "If you do these things, [then] yo never fall, and you will receive a rich welcome the eternal kingdom of our Lord and Savior Je

69

Christ" (2 Peter 1:10-11). What a powerful encouragement this is to those who sacrifice in this life to
prepare for the next. In heaven a great welcoming
committee awaits them, along with God's hearty
"Well done!" But this isn't automatic—the condi-
tional "if, then" makes it clear that if we don't do what
Peter prescribed, then we won't receive this rich
welcome when we enter heaven.

Where we spend eternity, whether heaven or hell,
depends on our faith. Our further condition in either
place will be determined by our works.

John Bunyan said, "Consider, to provoke you to
good works, that you shall have from God, when you
come to glory, a reward for everything you do for him
on earth."

A SECOND CHANCE?

My God-given resources, including money and
possessions, have immense potential. They are the
levers, positioned on the fulcrum of this life, by which
I can move the mountains of eternity.

Evangelicals reject the doctrine of a second chance
for unbelievers. We recognize that there's no opportunity to come to Christ after death. But it's equally
true that after death there's no second chance for
believers. There's no more opportunity for us to walk
by faith and serve our Lord in this fallen world.

We can't do life here over again. There's no retak-
ing the course once we've failed it. There's no
improving a D to an A. No rescheduling the final
exams. Death is the deadline. There's no extension.

A basketball game is over at the final buzzer. Shots taken late don't count. When the trumpet heralds Christ's return, our eternal future begins and our present opportunity ends. If we have failed by then to use our money, possessions, time, and energy for eternity, then we have failed—period.

"But we'll be in heaven and that's all that matters." On the contrary, Paul spoke of the loss of reward as a great and terrible loss. The fact that we're still saved is a clarification, not a consolation—"If it is burned up, he will suffer loss; he himself will be saved, but only as one escaping through the flames" (1 Corinthians 3:15). Receiving reward from Christ is an unspeakable gain with eternal implications. Forfeiting reward is a terrible loss with equally eternal implications.

How dare we say that being in heaven is all that matters to us, when so much else matters to God?

What we do in this life is of eternal importance. You and I will never have another chance to move the hand of God through prayer to heal a hurting soul, share Christ with one who can be saved from hell, care for the sick, serve a meal to the starving, comfort the dying, rescue the unborn, translate the Scriptures, bring the gospel to an unreached people group, further God's kingdom, open our homes, or share our clothes and food with the poor and needy.

What you do with your resources in this life is your autobiography. The book you've written with the pen of faith and the ink of works will go into eternity unedited, to be seen and read *as is* by the angels, the redeemed, and God himself. When we view today in light of the long tomorrow, the little choices become tremendously important. Whether I read my Bible today, pray, go to church, share my faith, and give my money—actions graciously empowered not by my flesh but by his Spirit—is of eternal consequence, not only for other souls, but for mine.

At death we put the signature to our life's portrait. The paint dries. The portrait's done. Ready or not.

Those who've dabbled in photography understand the "fixer." In developing a photograph, the negatives are immersed in different solutions. The developing solution parallels this life. As long as the photograph is in the developer it's subject to change. But once it's dropped into the fixer or "stop bath," it's permanently fixed. The photograph is done. What you see is what you get. So it will be when we die and enter eternity—the lives we lived on earth will be fixed as is, never to be altered or revised.

At the end of the movie *Schindler's List,* there's a heart-wrenching scene in which Oskar Schindler—who bought from the Nazis the lives of many Jews—looks at his car and his gold pin and regrets that he didn't give more of his money and possessions to save more lives. Schindler had used his opportunity far better than most. But in the end, he longed for a chance to go back and make better choices.

This life is our opportunity. Scripture does not teach what most of us seem to assume—that heaven will transform each of us into equal beings with equal possessions and equal responsibilities and equal capacities. It does not say our previous lives will be of no eternal significance. It says exactly the opposite.

Beyond the new heavens and new earth—which themselves are populated and structured according to what has been done in this life—there is no record of change. We might hope that what happens at the judgment seat will be of only temporary concern to the Judge, and that all of our disobedience and missed opportunities will make no difference. Will God make all souls equal in heaven and thereby consider as equally valid a life of selfishness and indifference to others' needs as compared to a life spent kneeling in prayer and feeding the hungry and sharing the gospel? The Bible clearly answers no.

PREPARING FOR THE FINAL EXAM

If we really believed that what we do with our money and possessions—and everything else—will have an irreversible effect on eternity . . . wouldn't we live differently?

There lies ahead for each of us, at the end of the term, a final examination. The potential rewards—and loss of rewards—on that day are inestimable. The test will be administered by a fair yet strict headmaster. How seriously we take this clear teaching of Scripture is demonstrated by how seriously we are preparing for that day.

When we took courses in college, we asked

questions about the teacher: "What are his tests like? Does he take attendance? Is he a hard grader? What does he expect in your papers?" If we're to do well in the course, we must know what the instructor expects of us.

We must study the course syllabus, God's Word, to find out the answers to these questions. Once we find out, we should be careful to plot our lives accordingly—in light of the long tomorrow.

I spent a day with a missionary friend in the ruins of ancient Corinth. For an hour we sat on the same judgment seat that Paul stood before in Acts 18, the one he used to help the Corinthians visualize Christ's future judgment of Christians. Together we read Scriptures that speak of that day when we will stand before the Lord's judgment seat and give an account for what we have done with all he has given us. We discussed the implications and prayed that when that day comes he might find us faithful and say to us, "Well done." We prayed knowing that our hourly and daily choices, empowered by our Lord, will determine what transpires on that day. It was one of the most sobering hours of my life.

When you leave this world, will you be known as one who accumulated treasures on earth that you couldn't keep? Or will you be recognized as one who invested treasures in heaven that you couldn't lose?

Martin Luther said that on his calendar there were only two days: "today" and "that Day." May we invest our money and possessions today in light of *that* day.

Alfred Nobel was a Swedish chemist who made his

fortune by inventing dynamite and other powerful explosives that governments bought to produce weapons. When Nobel's brother Ludvig died, a French newspaper accidentally printed Alfred's obituary instead. He was described as a man who became rich from enabling people to kill each other in unprecedented quantities. Shaken by this assessment, Nobel resolved to use his fortune to reward accomplishments that benefited humanity, including what we now know as the Nobel Peace Prize. He invested nine million dollars in this attempt to edit his role in history.

Nobel had a rare opportunity to look at the assessment of his life at its end—while he was still alive and had an opportunity to change that assessment.

Put yourself in Nobel's place. Read your own obituary, not as written by a reporter, but as an onlooking angel might write it from heaven's point of view. Look at it carefully.

Why not use the rest of your life to edit that obituary into what you want it to be?

CHAPTER 8

WELCOMED INTO HEAVEN'S HOMES

When I go to the grave I can say, as others have said, "My day's work is done." But I cannot say, "My life is done." My work will recommence the next morning. The tomb is not a blind alley; it is a thoroughfare. It closes upon the twilight but opens upon the dawn.
VICTOR HUGO

Christ's parable of the shrewd manager, often called the "unrighteous steward," is a powerful revelation about the eternal consequences of what we do with our money while on earth. However—largely due to our false assumptions about the eternal state—few who read the passage seem to grasp the points Jesus is making.

The parable concerns a wealthy owner who fires his business manager for wasting his assets (Luke 16:1-13). During the brief period before his termination is effective, the steward goes to his master's debtors and reduces their debt, thereby engendering their friendship and qualifying for their hospitality.

Despite the ethical issues, Jesus says, "The master commended the dishonest manager because he had acted shrewdly. For the people of this world are more shrewd in dealing with their own kind than are the people of the light." Jesus then adds this profound command to his disciples: "I tell you, use worldly wealth to gain friends for yourselves, so that when it is gone, you will be welcomed into eternal dwellings" (Luke 16:8-9).

Jesus does not endorse the man's ethics. Rather, he encourages us to follow the manager's example of using available resources to plan wisely for our futures.

We will be terminated from this life just as the shrewd steward was terminated from his job, and likely just as unexpectedly. As his master appointed a day for his service to end, so ours has chosen a day for our lives to end, when we will give an account of our stewardship. Worldly wealth will soon be gone. Before then, we should do exactly what this manager did—use wisely what little remaining time, influence, and financial resources we have before our term of stewardship is done.

Jesus doesn't tell us to stay away from the mammon of unrighteousness or "worldly wealth." He says to *use* it "to gain friends for yourselves, so that when it is gone, you will be welcomed into eternal dwellings" (Luke 16:9). Money can be a tool of Christ, but it must be used that way now. There's no second chance to use the money for Christ later. After his termination was effective, the steward would have no more leverage. He used his final days of service to win friends who could take him into their dwellings when his work was done.

After we die, Jesus is telling us, when our present

assets of money, possessions, time, and life are gone, we may be welcomed by friends into *eternal* dwellings.

Who are these friends? Apparently, people in heaven whom we touched in a significant way through the use of material assets on earth. Consequently, they will open to us their own "eternal dwelling places." The reference is plural, not singular—places, not place.

We don't get to heaven because we use money wisely. But we do gain access to other people's individual residences in heaven. Unlike the shrewd servant, Christians will have a wonderful place to live in heaven even without visiting others' dwellings. But like the shrewd steward, we will be welcomed into others' homes because we have used money and other resources to reach and serve them.

WELCOMED INTO LITERAL HOMES IN HEAVEN?
Many people take this passage figuratively. But why? The idea of believers having their own living quarters in heaven is corroborated by other texts. The New Jerusalem is a physical place, with exact measurements (Revelation 21:16). As a "city" it consists of individual residences (Revelation 21:2). Jesus stated that he's preparing for us eternal dwelling places on his master's estate (John 14:2-3).

First Corinthians 3:10-15 suggests that in this life we are providing the building materials for our Lord to use in this construction project. The size and quality of our eternal dwelling, then, may be influenced by how we live now. This fits the concept of reward commensurate to service taught in the judgment seat passages, as well as the stewardship parables.

If we follow through with the construction and residence imagery Scripture itself employs, then all believers are engaged in a sort of eternal building project, the results of which may vary widely. If we imagine angels employed by Jesus in our heavenly building projects, we might envision ourselves asking, "Why isn't my house larger than this?" Their response? "We did the best we could with what you sent us."

Based on Christ's words in the parable, we might further imagine that the larger our dwelling place, the more we will be able to serve as, so to speak, heavenly hosts—those who entertain heavenly guests. Perhaps we will even have angels as our guests. Or perhaps we may be invited into angels' quarters to visit with them in exchange for the hospitality we offered them on earth when we were unaware of their true identity (Hebrews 13:2)!

Does this seem fantastic? Or even offensive? I've found it troubles some people to think that service to people in this world will be rewarded by their hospitality to us in the next world. We act as if there is no continuity between our present lives on earth and our future lives in heaven. But there is.

Remember, I am simply trying to understand Christ's own words. I did not speak this parable. Jesus did. If he did not mean this, what did he mean? Since there is no indication that he was speaking symbolically or allegorically, shouldn't we take Christ's words in their plain and obvious sense?

Given the physical nature of our resurrection bodies and all that goes with it, including eating and drinking at tables together and living on a new earth in a great city, why should we be surprised to find that we will have actual places to live, or that we will be able to welcome others into them? If this sounds "too earthly," remember that the new earth, which will be the center of heaven itself (Revelation 21:1-2) is in fact a new *earth*—not a non-earth! Where do people with bodies live on earth? In dwelling places. Why should we be surprised at that idea in Luke 16, and why should we feel compelled not to take Christ's words at their face value?

This raises important questions. What kind of building materials are we sending ahead to heaven for our own dwelling place? Who have we influenced spiritually to the point that they would welcome us into their eternal dwelling places? To what needy people have we sacrificially given our resources?

Those whom we have influenced for Christ, directly or indirectly, will know and appreciate us and desire our fellowship in heaven. What a thought!

Ray Boltz's song "Thank You" pictures us meeting people in heaven who explain how our giving touched their lives. They say, "Thank you for giving to the Lord; I am so glad you gave." This is more than just a nice sentiment. It's something that will actually happen. Every time you give to your church, world missions, famine relief, and other kingdom causes, dream about

WHAT KIND OF BUILDING MATERIALS ARE WE SENDING AHEAD TO HEAVEN FOR OUR OWN DWELLING PLACE?

the day you will meet new friends in heaven and be welcomed by them into their homes.

In eternity we'll worship God with people of every tribe, nation, and language. We'll say thanks to them and they'll say thanks to us for acts of faithfulness done for Christ while we lived on earth. We'll tell our stories and listen to theirs, enjoying the warmth, sharing the joy, with our Lord the center of attention.

Do you have trouble getting out of bed in the morning? If picturing those scenes in heaven doesn't give you a purpose for living, I don't know what will!

Jesus gives us a powerful incentive to invest our lives and assets in his kingdom while on earth. The greater our service and sacrifice for him and for others, the larger and more enthusiastic our welcoming in heaven, the more substantial our own residences in heaven, and the more eternal dwellings we will have opportunity to visit.

One day our current money and possessions will be useless. While they're still useful, Christians with foresight will use them for eternal good.

TRUSTWORTHY WITH A LITTLE, ENTRUSTED WITH A LOT

Immediately after the parable of the shrewd manager, Jesus said, "Whoever can be trusted with very little can also be trusted with much, and whoever is dishonest with very little will also be dishonest with much" (Luke 16:10). God continually tests us in little things. (If a child can't be trusted to spend his father's money and return the change, neither can he be trusted to stay overnight alone at a friend's house.)

This invalidates all of our "if onlys," such as, "If only I made more money, then I'd help the poor," or "If only I had a million dollars, then I'd give it to my church or missions." If I'm dishonest or selfish in my use of a few dollars, I would be dishonest or selfish in my use of a million dollars. The issue is not what I would do with a million dollars if I had it, but what I am doing with the ten thousand, one thousand, one hundred, or ten dollars I *do* have. If we are not being faithful with what God has entrusted to us, why should he entrust us with any more?

This thought raises a sobering question: What opportunities are we currently missing because we've failed to use our money and our lives wisely in light of eternity?

What we do with a little time, a little talent, and a little money tells God—and our family and friends and world—a great deal.

HANDLING TRUE RICHES

"So if you have not been trustworthy in handling worldly wealth, who will trust you with true riches?" (Luke 16:11). What are "true riches"? They're not just more of the same worldly wealth. True riches are what's valuable to God, what will last for all eternity. What could those be but other human beings with eternal souls? Apparently God tests us in the handling of money and possessions to determine our trustworthiness in personal ministry.

Through mismanagement of God's funds we can lose credibility with people as well as God's willingness to entrust us with more. Having been faithful in handling our resources in this life, we are granted leadership of others in the next life (Luke 19:17, 19).

"And if you have not been trustworthy with someone else's property, who will give you property of your own?" (Luke 16:12). This passage implies that though we are currently stewards, we will someday be property owners if we are faithful with his resources on earth. Jesus confirmed this when he spoke of storing up for ourselves treasures in heaven. We will have ownership of treasures in heaven that he allowed us to send on ahead so they'd be waiting for us.

Now think about *that* for a few million years!

FIELD TRIP TO A JUNKYARD

Gather your family and go visit a junkyard or a dump. Look at all the piles of "treasures" that were formerly Christmas and birthday presents. Point out things that people worked long hours to buy and paid hundreds of dollars for, that children quarreled about, friendships were lost over, honesty was sacrificed for, and marriages broke up over. Look at the remnants of gadgets and furnishings that now lie useless after their brief life span. Remind yourself that most of what you own will one day end up in a junkyard like this. And even if it survives on earth for a while, you won't.

When you examine the junkyard, ask yourself this question: "When all that I ever owned lies abandoned, broken, useless, and forgotten, what will I have done with my life that will last for eternity? Who will welcome me into their eternal dwelling places because God used me to touch their lives?"

CHAPTER 9

FROM HERE TO ETERNITY'S REWARDS

It is my happiness that I have served Him who never fails to reward His servants to the full extent of His promise.
JOHN CALVIN

Two men owned farms side by side. One was a bitter atheist, the other a devout Christian. Constantly annoyed at the Christian for his trust in God, the atheist said to him one winter, "Let's plant our crops as usual this spring, each the same number of acres. You pray to your God, and I'll curse him. Then come October, let's see who has the bigger crop."

When October came the atheist was delighted because his crop was larger. "See, you fool," he taunted, "what do you have to say for your God now?"

"My God," replied the other farmer, "doesn't settle all his accounts in October."

A CLOSER LOOK AT REWARDS

A day of judgment is coming upon all men. God promises great reward for all who have served him faithfully. He will reward every loyal servant for works done in this life: "At that time each will receive his praise from God" (1 Corinthians 4:5). This is a particularly encouraging passage, suggesting that God will find something to praise and reward each one of us for. Shouldn't that motivate us to do more for our Father that he will take pleasure in and be proud of?

God rewards generously, promising a return of "a hundred times" (Matthew 19:29). This is ten thousand percent interest, a return far out of proportion to the amount invested. No earthly investment will pay such dividends, and even if it did, they wouldn't last.

WHAT DOES GOD REWARD?

According to the Bible, God rewards for many things, including doing good works (Ephesians 6:8; Romans 2:6, 10), denying ourselves (Matthew 16:24-27), showing compassion to the needy (Luke 14:13-14), and treating our enemies kindly (Luke 6:35). He also grants us rewards for sacrificial and generous giving: "Go, sell your possessions and give to the poor, and you will have treasure in heaven" (Matthew 19:21).

God promises rewards to those who endure difficult circumstances while trusting him (Hebrews 10:34-36), to those who live faithfully and with good motives (1 Corinthians 4:2,5), and to those who persevere under persecution (Luke 6:22-23). God will richly reward a life of godliness (2 Peter 3:11-14).

God will also reward those who make wise and productive use of the resources and opportunities he has given them (Matthew 25:14-23).

Paul reminds us there's a timetable for the harvest: "Let us not become weary in doing good, for at the proper time we will reap a harvest if we do not give up"

(Galatians 6:9). Like the law of gravity, the law of rewards—the law of the harvest—is always in effect, even when we can't see it. Everything and everyone in human history is headed toward a day of reaping, even if it does not seem obvious. The farmer should not be discouraged and give up his work if the crop growth seems indiscernible day to day. Likewise, the Christian's persistent faith, refusing to give up, trusts God that the harvest will come, and at just the right time.

GOD'S WORDS AS A GUIDE

"Honor the Lord with your wealth, with the firstfruits of all your crops." (Proverbs 3:9)

"Command those who are rich in this present world not to be arrogant nor to put their hope in wealth, which is so uncertain, but to put their hope in God, who richly provides us with everything for our enjoyment. Command them to do good, to be rich in good deeds, and to be generous and willing to share. In this way they will lay up treasure for themselves as a firm foundation for the coming age, so that they may take hold of the life that is truly life." (1 Timothy 6:17-19)

Prosperity theology gets it right that God rewards faithfulness but gets it wrong when it comes to the location and timing of rewards. It assumes rewards are here and now, while Scripture teaches us that the greatest rewards will be not here and now but then and there.

We're told, "Everyone who wants to live a godly life in Christ Jesus will be persecuted" (2 Timothy 3:12). In the short term, this teaches exactly the opposite of prosperity theology. But in the long term we are always promised that obedience brings eternal rewards that far exceed any temporary hardship:

> Therefore we do not lose heart. Though outwardly we are wasting away, yet inwardly we are being renewed day by day. For our light and momentary troubles are achieving for us an eternal glory that far outweighs them all. So we fix our eyes not on what is seen, but on what is unseen. For what is seen is temporary, but what is unseen is eternal. (2 Corinthians 4:16-18)

The believer's compensation, just like the unbeliever's, is usually deferred. Our God doesn't settle all his accounts in October.

THE REWARD OF RULERSHIP

Believers will reign with Christ over the world (Revelation 20:6). We'll even rule over angels (1 Corinthians 6:3). Some will be put "in charge of many things" (Matthew 25:21-23). Christ spoke of granting some followers rulership over cities—eleven cities for one, five for another, and none for a third, in proportion to their faithful service (Luke 19:17-24).

It's apparent from these passages that although all believers will be with Christ, not all will reign with him, at least not with equal responsibility and authority.

There are stated conditions for reigning: "If we endure, we will also reign with him" (2 Timothy 2:12). Christ promises, "To him who overcomes, I will give the right to sit with me on my throne" (Revelation 3:21). He says, "To him who overcomes and does my will to the end, I will give authority over the nations . . . just as I have received authority from my Father. I will also give him the morning star" (Revelation 2:26-28).

CROWNS AS REWARDS

Crowns are a common symbol of ruling power, though they may symbolize other rewards as well. Five crowns are mentioned in the New Testament:

1. The crown of life—given for faithfulness to Christ in persecution or martyrdom (James 1:12; Revelation 2:10).
2. The incorruptible crown—given for determination, discipline, and victory in the Christian life (1 Corinthians 9:24-25).
3. The crown of rejoicing—given for pouring oneself into others in evangelism and discipleship (1 Thessalonians 2:19; Philippians 4:1).
4. The crown of glory—given for faithfully representing Christ in a position of spiritual leadership (1 Peter 5:1-4). (Note that a prerequisite is being "not greedy for money, but eager to serve." A Christian leader's preoccupation with money can forfeit this reward.)
5. The crown of righteousness—given for joyfully purifying and readying oneself to meet Christ at his return (2 Timothy 4:6-8).

There's nothing in this list that suggests it's exhaustive. There may be innumerable crowns and types of crowns and rewards unrelated to crowns. But all are graciously given by the Lord Jesus in response to the faithful efforts of the believer, which themselves are empowered by God's grace.

These crowns bring glory to Christ as they are laid before his feet (Revelation 4:10), showing that our rewards are given not merely for our recognition but for God's glory. Although God's glory is the highest reason for any action, Scripture sees no contradiction between God's eternal glory and our eternal good. On the contrary, glorifying God will always result in our greatest eternal good. Likewise, pursuing our eternal good, as he commands us to do, will always glorify God.

False humility says, "I want no reward." Effectively that means, "I want nothing to lay at Christ's feet to bring him glory." We may think we are taking the spiritual high ground by being disinterested in rewards, but this is foreign to Scripture. Of course we should desire rewards. Hearing our Master say, "Well done" will not simply be for our pleasure but for *his!*

We are to guard our crowns carefully (Revelation 3:11). Why? Because we can be disqualified from receiving them (1 Corinthians 9:27). We can lose them (1 Corinthians 3:15). They can be taken from us (Matthew 25:28-29). We can seek our rewards from men, thereby forfeiting them from God (Matthew

6:5-6). John warns, "Watch out that you do not lose what you have worked for, but that you may be rewarded fully" (2 John 8). We can fail to gain rewards, and we can forfeit rewards already in our account.

ETERNAL DIFFERENCES IN HEAVEN?

Not all Christians will hear the master say, "Well done, good and faithful servant" (Matthew 25:23). Not all of us will have treasure in heaven (Matthew 6:19-21). Not all of us will have the same position of authority in heaven (Luke 19:17, 19, 26). We will have differing rewards in heaven (1 Corinthians 3:12-15), depending on our actions and choices here on earth. There is no hint that, once given or withheld, rewards are anything other than eternal and irrevocable.

> **REWARD PRINCIPLE #6: WE WILL HAVE DIFFERING LEVELS OF REWARD IN HEAVEN, DEPENDING ON OUR ACTIONS AND CHOICES ON EARTH.**

Scripture suggests that some Christians will be ashamed at Christ's coming (1 John 2:28). Although it seems incomprehensible that such shame would continue in heaven, the doctrine of eternal rewards certainly has sobering implications. The tangible results of those who have faithfully served Christ in this life and those who haven't will be evident for all eternity. They will be exemplified in eternal possessions (treasures) and positions (rulership) that will differ significantly from person to person.

Scripture is clear that there's a payback in eternity according to what was done during our time on earth, and there will be commensurate differences in our rewards (Proverbs 24:12; Matthew 19:27-30; Luke 14:12-14). In other words, our experiences in heaven will not be identical. (Obviously, in heaven there will be no conceit, pettiness, jealousy, or unhealthy comparisons, but there nonetheless will be differences in reward and position.)

We saw earlier that hell will be terrible for all, but it will be more terrible for some than others, depending on their works on earth (Matthew 11:20-24; Luke 20:45-47). Doesn't it follow that although everyone's experience in heaven will be wonderful, it will be more wonderful for some than others, depending on their service for Christ while on earth?

Perhaps it's a matter of differing capacities. Two jars can both be full, but the one with greater capacity contains more. Likewise, all of us will be full of joy in heaven, but some may have more joy because their capacity for joy will be larger, having been stretched through trusting God in this life.

John Bunyan put it this way:

> And why shall he that doth most for God in this world, enjoy most of him in that which is to come? But because by doing and acting, the heart, and every faculty of the soul is enlarged, and more capacitated, whereby more room is made for glory. . . . He that is best bred, and that is most in the bosom of God, and that so

acts for him here; he is the man that will be best able to enjoy most of God in the kingdom of heaven.[10]

No matter how we attempt to explain it, no matter how uneasy it makes us, it's a fact that the biblical doctrine of differing rewards and differing positions in heaven means we will have different experiences in heaven. These eternal experiences are presently being forged in the crucible of this life. Even if I cannot yet comprehend how, the fact remains that what I do with my money and possessions here and now will significantly affect my eternal experience in heaven.

UNDERSTANDING SALVATION AND REWARDS

Whenever we speak of rewards, particularly because we speak of them so rarely, it's easy to confuse God's work and man's. Many mistakenly believe that heaven is our reward for doing good things. This is absolutely not the case. Our presence in heaven is in no sense a reward for our works, but a gift freely given by God in response to faith, which is itself God's gift (Romans 6:23; Ephesians 2:8-9; Titus 3:5).

For Christians, salvation took place in a moment in the past. It was free, it can't be lost, it is the same for all Christians, and it is for those who believe. By contrast, rewards will be given in the future, are earned (by God's grace), can be lost, differ among Christians, and are for those who work.

Salvation	Rewards
Past (1 John 3:2)	Future (Rev. 22:12)
Free (Eph. 2:8-9)	Earned (1 Cor. 3:8)
Can't be lost (John 10:28-29)	Can be lost (2 John 1:8)
Same for all Christians (Rom. 3:22)	Differ among Christians (1 Cor. 3:12-15)
For those who believe (John 3:16)	For those who work (1 Cor. 9:27)

Salvation is about God's work for us. Conversely, rewards are a matter of *our* work for God. When it comes to salvation, our work for God is no substitute for God's work for us. God *saves* us because of *Christ's* work, not ours. Likewise, when it comes to rewards, God's work for us is no substitute for our work for God. God *rewards* us for *our* work, not Christ's. (Of course, it is *empowered* by Christ, but God nevertheless refers to it as our work.)

Let me be sure this is perfectly clear. Christ paid the eternal price (hell) for all our sins, once and for all (Hebrews 10:12-18). If we have trusted him for that provision, we will not pay the eternal price; that is, we will not go to hell. He has fully forgiven our sins and we are completely secure in the love of Christ (Psalm 103:8-18; Romans 8:31-39). Our salvation is sure, and we will not undergo the judgment of condemnation (John 5:24; Romans 8:1).

But although the forgiveness of our sins has every bearing on our eternal destination, it has no automatic bearing on our eternal rewards. The Bible teaches not only forgiveness of our sins but also consequences of our choices. These consequences apply despite our forgiveness. Forgiveness means that God eliminates our eternal condemnation. But it does not

mean that our actions in this life have no consequences on earth. (Forgiven people can still contract AIDS, go to jail for drunk driving, or suffer the death penalty, for example.)

Neither does it mean our choices have no consequences in eternity. Forgiven people can still lose their rewards and forfeit eternal positions of responsibility they could have had if they'd served Christ on earth.

With our salvation, the work was Christ's. With our rewards, the work is ours. It's imperative that we trust in Christ, lean on him, and draw upon him for power, for apart from him we can do nothing. But if we hope to receive a reward, we must still do the necessary work. As our forefathers put it, we must bear the cross if we are to wear the crown.

Belief (trust, faith) determines our eternal destination: *where* we will be. Behavior (obedience, works) determines our eternal rewards: *what* we will have there. Works do not affect our destination, since our redemption is secured by the work of Christ. However, works *do* affect our reward experienced at that destination.

Just as there are eternal consequences to our faith, so there are eternal consequences to our works.

What we do with our resources—including our time, money, and possessions—will matter not just twenty minutes, twenty days, or twenty years from now. It will matter twenty *trillion* years from now.

This is God's law of rewards. The more we come to grips with it, the more we glorify the one who designed this law and who sees that it is always carried out.

CHAPTER 10

REWARDS: OUR MISSING MOTIVATION

Whatever good thing you do for Him, if done according to the Word, is laid up for you as treasure in chests and coffers, to be brought out to be rewarded before both men and angels, to your eternal comfort.

JOHN BUNYAN

"Why should I follow Scripture's teaching on money and possessions when it's so much fun to have all the nice things I want and do whatever I please with my money? I'm a Christian, and I know I'm going to heaven anyway, so why get radical about the whole money thing? Why not have the best of both worlds, this one and the next?"

Though few of us are bold enough to openly ask such questions, they accurately reflect our underlying attitude.

A STEWARD'S MOTIVATION

The missing ingredient in the lives of countless Christians today is *motivation*. Given our false assumption that what we do in this life won't have eternal consequences—apart from our decision to place our trust in Christ for salvation—it's no wonder we're unmotivated to follow God's directions regarding money and possessions, giving, or anything else. When it comes down to it, what difference will it make? According to the prevailing evangelical theology, everything comes out in the wash, so it won't make any difference at all. But according to the Bible, it will make a tremendous difference! The doctrine of eternal rewards for our obedience is the neglected key to unlocking our motivation.[11]

Moses "regarded disgrace for the sake of Christ as of greater value than the treasures of Egypt, because . . ." Stop right there. Because *why?* Now read the rest: "because he was looking ahead to his reward" (Hebrews 11:26). Motivated by long-term reward, he chose short-term disgrace. Not because he wanted disgrace, but because he wanted reward!

This prospect of eternal reward from his Master's hand was Paul's consuming motivation throughout his life:

> Do you not know that in a race all the runners run, but only one gets the prize? Run in such a way as to get the prize. Everyone who competes in the games goes into strict training. They do it to get a crown that will not last; but we do it to get a crown that will last forever. Therefore I do not run like a man running aimlessly; I do not fight like a man beating the air. No, I beat my body and make it my slave so that after I have preached to others, I myself will not be disqualified for the prize. (1 Corinthians 9:24-27)

Yes, Paul recognized there was a price that must be paid to follow Christ with discipline and faithfulness. But he was willing to pay the price because of the prize. He recognized the law of rewards, and he gladly sacrificed lesser treasures that wouldn't last for greater treasures that would last.

Paul was unashamedly motivated by the prospect of eternal reward right until the day he died. At the very end of his life, knowing he was about to be executed under Nero, he said, "I have fought the good fight, I have finished the race, I have kept the faith. Now there is in store for me the crown of righteousness, which the Lord, the righteous Judge, will award to me on that day—and not only to me, but also to all who have longed for his appearing" (2 Timothy 4:7-8).

Paul encouraged all believers to be motivated by rewards (Galatians 6:9-10; 1 Timothy 6:17-19). He told slaves to obey their masters in order to receive eternal reward: "Serve wholeheartedly, as if you were serving the Lord, not men, because you know that the Lord will reward everyone for whatever good he does, whether he is slave or free" (Ephesians 6:7-8).

Christ himself was motivated not only by love but also by reward. He endured the cross "for the joy set before him" (Hebrews 12:2). He humbled himself, knowing that he would ultimately be exalted (Philippians 2:9).

Jesus said, "But when you give a banquet, invite the poor, the crippled, the lame, the blind, and you will be blessed. Although they cannot repay you, you will be repaid at the resurrection of the righteous"

THE DOCTRINE OF ETERNAL REWARDS FOR OUR OBEDIENCE IS THE NEGLECTED KEY TO UNLOCKING OUR MOTIVATION. (Luke 14:13-14). Our instinct is to give to those who will give us something in return and not to give to those who won't. Christ appealed not only to our compassion but also to our self-interest. *If we do a compassionate act that goes unrewarded by others in this life, God will pay us back in the next life.* This gives us an extra incentive to help the helpless. Not only do they need our help, not only does it please God, but he is eager to reward us for it!

What a motivation this is when we feel our labors are unappreciated by others! We can be delivered from the burden of concern about whether others overlook our deeds, because God assures us that he will not overlook them. When we understand what it means to be promised a reward from God, any prospect of reward from others—or any bitterness for not being rewarded by them—will shrink in comparison.

There's a story about a man and his wife who returned to America after many years as missionaries in Africa. This was before airplanes, back when the voyage was by ship and took months. When the ship finally docked in a U.S. harbor, the couple heard cheering from the shore. For a moment their hearts were lifted. But soon they realized the cheering was for a Hollywood actor onboard their ship. There was no one to meet them. The man was very discouraged and struggled with bitterness. He lamented, "After all these years serving God, after all the sacrifices, there's no one to greet us? *This* is our homecoming?" His wife squeezed his hand and said, "We're not home yet."

We shouldn't expect a great homecoming until we really arrive home. God will be in charge of that party! And if we've served him here, his welcome will be glorious.

"Love your enemies, and do good, and lend, expecting nothing in return; and your reward will be great, and you will be sons of the Most High" (Luke 6:35, NASB). We are to expect nothing in return from people, knowing that we will receive a far greater reward in return from God's gracious hand.

REWARD PRINCIPLE #7: DESIRING REWARDS IS A PROPER MOTIVATION FOR SERVING CHRIST.

Despite prevailing opinions to the contrary, the prospect of rewards is a proper motivation for the Christian's obedience—including the generous sharing of our money and possessions. If we maintain that it's wrong to be motivated by rewards, we bring a serious accusation against Christ. We imply he is tempting us to sin every time he offers rewards for obedience! When he offered us treasures for ourselves in heaven, was he tempting us toward sin? If rewards are a wrong motive, then he was luring us to do wrong. This is unthinkable. Since God does not tempt his children, it's clear that whatever he lays before us as a motivation is legitimate. It's not wrong for us to be motivated by the prospect of reward. Indeed, something is seriously wrong if we are *not* motivated by the promise of reward made by our God.

THE POWER OF INCENTIVES

Businesspeople work in a world of incentives. So do homemakers, schoolchildren, and every other human being, regardless of age, nationality, or wealth. Every effective manager, every wise leader knows the importance of incentives. These are tangible motivators that may be personal, social, spiritual, physical, or financial. Unfortunately, too many Christians consider incentives to be "secular," "carnal," or "unspiritual."

Most of us use rewards to motivate our children. So why are we surprised that God uses rewards to motivate us? By God's own design, *all* of us need incentives to motivate us to do our jobs and do them well. Motivation by reward is not a result of the fall. Rather, it is God's original design for humanity.

To say, "I don't do anything for the reward—I do it only because it's right," may appear to take the spiritual high road. But in fact it's pseudospiritual. It goes against the grain of the way God created us and the way he himself motivates us. And it completely contradicts all the passages of Scripture that clearly attempt to motivate us by our desire for rewards. When we say, "You shouldn't do anything to get a reward," do we imagine we are more spiritual than Jesus, Paul, and God's Word?

When our daughters lived in our home as teenagers, suppose I'd told one of them, "If you do a full day of yard work Saturday, I'll pay you fifty dollars and take you out to a nice dinner." Would it be wrong for her to want to earn the fifty dollars? Would it be wrong for her to look forward to going out to a nice dinner with her dad? Of course it wouldn't be wrong! I'm her father, I made the offer, and I *want* her to want those things!

Of course, it would be inappropriate if my daughter refused to work unless I offered her rewards. But because rewarding her was my idea, not hers, she would have every right to be motivated by the rewards I offered her. In fact, my own joy would be lessened if she *didn't* want the rewards I offered her—especially the reward of enjoying that special dinner together.

"But God doesn't owe us anything," you might argue. "He has the right to expect us to work for him with no thought of reward." True, we should be willing and happy to serve him, even if there was no payoff. Jesus addressed this when he said, "So you also, when you have done everything you were told to do, should say, 'We are unworthy servants; we have only done our duty' " (Luke 17:10).

The point is, God owes us nothing. So if we came to him and said, "You owe us—we want to be paid," we would be dead wrong.

But here's the incredible thing, the factor that turns the entire debate on its head—it wasn't *our* idea that God would reward us. It was *his* idea! Satan didn't make up the idea of incentives. Our sin nature didn't make it up. A corrupt world didn't make it up. *God* made it up. He designed us to need incentives to motivate us to do our jobs and do them well.

Suppose my daughter did the yard work joylessly and then said, "Dad, I just did my duty. I refuse the money, and I don't want to go to dinner with you." How would that make me feel?

We flatter ourselves—and insult God—when we say, "I don't care about reward."

God will reward the child who gave to the missions offering the money she'd saved for a softball mitt. He'll reward the teenager who kept himself pure despite all the temptations. He'll reward the man who tenderly cared for his wife with Alzheimer's, the mother who raised the child with cerebral palsy, the child who rejoiced despite his handicap. He'll reward the unskilled person who was faithful and the skilled person who was meek and servant-hearted. He'll reward the parents who modeled Christ to their children and the children who followed him despite their parents' bad example. He'll reward those who suffered while trusting him, and those who helped the ones who were suffering. He'll reward the couple who downsized, selling their large house to live in a small one and give all the money away to missions.

He doesn't *have* to reward anyone for anything. He does it because he *wants* to! And make no mistake: regardless of what you and I think about it, that's exactly what he's going to do. "For the Son of Man is going to come in his Father's glory with his angels, and then he will reward each person *according to what he has done*" (Matthew 16:27, italics mine).

Why does God reward us? Because he is pleased by what we've done. A child who wants to be rewarded by his parents realizes they will be pleased by his good deeds. Hence, his desire for reward is not mercenary—it is inseparable from his love for his parents and his desire for their approval.

CHOICES AND CONSEQUENCES

Every major choice involves major consequences. Scripture brims with promises and warnings of the consequences for our choices—this punishment for that sin, that reward for this obedience.

Of course, reward is not our only motivation. We should be motivated by gratitude to serve God (Hebrews 12:28). We should be motivated by our ambition "to please him" (2 Corinthians 5:9). But these motives are never in scriptural conflict with the motive of reward. The same Bible that calls upon us to obey God out of our love for him as Father and Redeemer (Deuteronomy 7:9; 11:1; 30:20) also calls upon us to obey out of our fear of him as Creator and Judge (Genesis 2:17; Deuteronomy 28:58-67; Hebrews 10:30-31) and out of our hope in him as Rewarder (Deuteronomy 28:2-9; Hebrews 11:6). Each of these motivations is legitimate, and each complements the other.

Sometimes we need the combined persuasiveness of all these incentives to do what is pleasing to the Lord. This isn't a matter of *mixed* motives (some good, some bad) but of *multiple* motives—multiple *righteous* motives.

We should evangelize out of our love for God. But
if that isn't enough, our love for other people should
motivate us. Scripture tells us we should also be motivated to evangelize out of our fear of God. We will
stand before the judgment seat and be recompensed
for our works, Paul says, adding, "Since, then, we know
what it is to fear the Lord, we try to persuade men"
(2 Corinthians 5:10-11). Love is one motivator. Fear is
another. Reward is another. If one or two of these
motives don't seem enough, the three together should.

Our delightful daughters are grown and married
now. When they were children, they loved their
mother and me, and sometimes that was a sufficient
incentive for obeying. But other times it wasn't
enough. Fortunately, they also feared me, in the best
sense. They knew I would punish wrongdoing. And
they also knew I'd be very pleased when they did the
right thing. They knew I would reward them for doing
right, always with approving words, and sometimes
in material ways too.

What is in God's best interests is also in others'
best interests and in my best interests (not necessar-
ily immediately, but always ultimately). Something
that is good will always be good for everyone—not
good for God and bad for me, or good for me and bad
for my neighbor. What's good is good for all. Every
time I obey God, I'm doing what's ultimately best for
everyone. Each time I disobey him, I'm doing what's
ultimately worst for everyone. The Master and steward are both pleased when the steward does well.
Both are displeased when he doesn't do well.

Praise is a strong motivator. Children are motivated by the hope of being praised by their parents. Why would it be different with God's children? The prospect of hearing my Father say to me, "Well done" should be tremendously motivating. The Pharisees "loved praise from men more than praise from God" (John 12:43). Their problem wasn't that they were motivated by praise. It's that they were working for praise from the wrong source—men, rather than God.

How should we respond to adversity for the sake of Christ? "Rejoice in that day and leap for joy." *Why* should we leap for joy? Because we're masochists? No. "Because great is your reward in heaven" (Luke 6:23).

The believer who knows God's Word knows its promise of reward for obedience. God has set up a system that rewards obedience and punishes disobedience. He rewards others-centered sacrifice and punishes self-centered indulgence. What's right is always smart, because it will be rewarded. What's wrong is always stupid, because it will be punished. This is the way God has made things. This system—not our personal preferences—should be our reference point in deciding what to do with our lives, our time, and our money and possessions.

If we don't recognize God's law of rewards, if we fail to live by it, we lose. It's that simple. We miss out on eternal benefits he freely offered us and wanted us to have. If we do live by the law of rewards, it's equally simple. He is always pleased, and we always come out ahead . . . forever.

CHAPTER 11

POWER, PLEASURES, AND POSSESSIONS: TEMPTATIONS OR MOTIVATIONS?

Where riches hold the dominion of the heart,
God has lost His authority.

JOHN CALVIN

God has created us each with desires for pleasure, possessions, and power. He has built us to be motivated by these desires.

At first this may sound unbiblical, because we've come to think of these things as temptations, not legitimate motivations. Satan does indeed tempt us in each of these areas. The desire for pleasure can and often does degenerate into hedonism, desire for possessions into materialism, and desire for power into egotism. We might relate the desire for pleasure to the "lust of the flesh," the desire for possessions to the "lust of the eyes," and the desire for power to "the pride of life" (1 John 2:16, KJV).

Satan approached Christ on all three of these levels during his wilderness temptation. He tempted Jesus to make bread for the *pleasure* of eating, to worship Satan for the *possession* of all the world's kingdoms, and to cast himself from the highest point of the temple for the *power* of commanding angelic intervention (Luke 4:1-13).

So if the desires for pleasure, possessions, and power make us vulnerable to temptation, how can they be good? How can they properly motivate us?

GOD'S WORDS AS A GUIDE

"Whoever trusts in his riches will fall, but the righteous will thrive like a green leaf." (Proverbs 11:28)

"Rich and poor have this in common: The Lord is the Maker of them all." (Proverbs 22:2)

We must understand that the evil one can appeal to our desires for these things *only because our Creator built those desires into us.*

The draw to pleasure, possessions, and power cannot be rooted in our sin nature. Why do I say that? Because Satan appealed to these desires in Adam and Eve *before they ever sinned* (Genesis 3:1-7). But there's further proof. Christ had no sin nature. Satan knew this, yet he sought to tempt Jesus on these same three grounds—pleasure, possessions, and power. Why? Because Christ was not only God but man, and to be human is to have desires for these things. We want pleasure, possessions, and power not because we are sinful but *because we are human.*

If this argument seems unconvincing, there's a

clincher: the simple reality that God himself appeals to each of these desires in us! He offers us the reward of power in his eternal kingdom (Matthew 20:20-28; Luke 12:42-44; 19:15-19), possessions in his eternal kingdom (Matthew 6:19-21; 19:16-22, 27-30), and pleasures in his eternal kingdom (Psalm 16:11).

God appeals to our human nature but *never* to our sin nature. Power, possessions, and pleasures are legitimate objects of desire that our Creator has instilled in us *and* by which he can motivate us to obedience. The evil one counterattacks by tempting us to direct these legitimate desires to the wrong objects, in the wrong time or wrong place—or by convincing us that it is never right to desire such things even when God himself offers them.

GAINING ETERNAL PLEASURE, POSSESSIONS, AND POWER

The devil tempts us to idolize pleasure, possessions, and power and pursue them in the present world. The Lord's desire is that we seek to gain these things in the future—not by clinging to them in the present but by *forgoing* them in the present.

> **REWARD PRINCIPLE #8: WE ARE NOT TO BE MOTIVATED PRIMARILY BY EARTHLY POWER, POSSESSIONS, AND PLEASURES, YET WE ARE OFFERED ALL THREE IN HEAVEN IF WE INVEST NOW IN GOD'S KINGDOM.**

Consider the threefold disciplines of fasting, giving, and prayer, which Christ addresses in Matthew 6:1-18. Fasting is denying ourselves the pleasure of eating in order to gain pleasure in God. Giving is denying the possession of riches to gain possessions from God. Prayer is denying our own power in order to gain power from God. Eating, owning, and ruling are not bad—but we temporarily abstain from them, as a matter of spiritual discipline, in order to accomplish a higher kingdom purpose.

For centuries, monastic orders have tried to practice relinquishment through their vow of chastity (forgoing pleasure), vow of poverty (forgoing possessions), and vow of obedience (forgoing the power of living life one's own way).

But one need not forgo power because he hates power. He may forgo it now precisely because he wants it in a better world. Jesus didn't tell his disciples they shouldn't want to be great. Rather, he told them how they could become great in the next world—by being a servant in this one (Mark 10:42-44).

Likewise, one does not forgo possessions here because he hates possessions, but because he wants them in another world. Jesus didn't tell his disciples they shouldn't want to be rich. Rather, he told them they could become rich in the next world by giving away riches in this one, thereby laying up treasures for themselves in heaven (Matthew 6:19-21). It's not a matter of no gratification but delayed gratification.

It's forgoing present, temporal gratification in order to achieve future, eternal gratification.

We admire Olympic athletes for their dedication and discipline, but we don't imagine they're not acting from self-interest, do we?

FAITH IS WHAT MOTIVATES US TO FORGO SOMETHING IN THIS LIFE FOR THE PROMISE THAT IT—OR SOMETHING EVEN BETTER— WILL BE OURS IN THE NEXT.

We're right to admire a missionary, someone who works with street children, or someone who feeds the poor. Yet what they are doing is not selfless in the full sense of the term. Their short-term sacrifices are in their eternal self-interest, because God promises to reward them. This is not self-denial for its own sake, but purposeful self-denial for God's glory and their own ultimate good. The key to this self-denial is faith, as described and exemplified in Hebrews 11:8-16. Faith is what motivates us to forgo something in this life for the promise that it—or something even better—will be ours in the next life.

This concept is difficult for us to understand, because our sin nature has so tainted our pleasures, possessions, and power in this world. But in eternity we'll be able to manage these things rightly—as our sinless Lord did—because we'll be without sin. There will be no curse on the new earth, and no curse means no sin (Revelation 22:3).

Our love for responsibility (power), treasures (possessions), and sensory delights (pleasures) will be righteous, not tainted in the slightest by sin.

CAN APPEAL TO OUR DESIRES REALLY BE SPIRITUAL?

God created us with certain desires, and he made us to be motivated by rewards that appeal to those desires. He calls us to act on the basis of those promised rewards. As we've seen, the Scriptures are full of exhortations to act in certain ways to gain certain rewards. Yet there persists a misguided belief that desire for power, possessions, and pleasure in the next life is crass and to pursue rewards is selfish or mercenary.

It is certainly true that desire for reward should not be our *only* motivation. But it is also true that it's a fully legitimate motive encouraged by God. In fact, the two most basic things we can believe about God are first that he exists, and second that *he is a rewarder* of those who diligently seek him (Hebrews 11:6). If you don't believe God is a rewarder, you are rejecting a major biblical doctrine and have a false view of God. I encourage you to go back to the Scriptures and ask God to open your eyes to the truth about his nature and how he motivates his people.

Jesus commands us to do what's in our own best interest, to store up *for ourselves* treasures in heaven. Is that selfish? No. God expects and commands us to act out of enlightened self-interest. Our generosity is not only for God's glory, not only for others' good, but also for *our* good. One of Satan's great lies, believed by many Christians, is that we must choose between doing what honors Christ and doing what's best for us! In fact, they are one and the same.

Selfishness is when we pursue gain at the expense of others. But God doesn't have a limited number of treasures to distribute. When you store up treasures for yourself in heaven, it doesn't reduce the treasures available to others. In fact, it's by serving God and others that we store up heavenly treasures. This is God's law of rewards. Everyone gains; no one loses.

The devil desperately tries to defame the very rewards God the loving father graciously offers his children. God wants us to want these rewards. Satan wants us to not want them.

INSTRUCTION FROM THREE ENGLISH CHRISTIANS

Three godly Englishmen of three different centuries offer us an explicitly biblical perspective on this question.

John Bunyan, the seventeenth-century pastor who was imprisoned for preaching the gospel, said of eternal rewards, "They are such as should make us leap to think on, and that we should remember with exceeding joy, and never think that it is contrary to the Christian faith, to rejoice and be glad for [them]."[12]

William Wilberforce, through his tireless efforts in Parliament in the early nineteenth century, finally succeeded in abolishing England's slave trade. He devoted most of his fortune to the cause of Christ. This was his perspective on our God-given desires: "Christianity proposes not to extinguish our natural desires. It promises to bring the desires under just control and direct them to their true object."[13]

C. S. Lewis, a professor at Oxford and Cambridge in the mid-twentieth century, wrote prolifically on the Christian faith. He diverted most of his royalties to charitable causes and individual needs, living simply and thinking often of the next world:

> The New Testament has lots to say about self-denial, but not about self-denial as an end in itself. We are told to deny ourselves and to take up our cross in order that we may follow Christ—and nearly every description of what we shall ultimately find if we do so contains an appeal to desire. If there lurks in most modern minds the notion that it's a bad thing to desire our own good and earnestly to hope for the enjoyment of it is a bad thing, I submit that this notion has crept in from the teachings of Kant and the Stoics and is no part of the Christian faith. Indeed, if we consider the unblushing promises of rewards and the staggering nature of the rewards promised in the Gospels, it would seem that our Lord finds our desires not too strong, but too weak. We are half-hearted creatures, fooling about with drink and sex and ambition when infinite joy is offered us, like an ignorant child who goes on making mud pies in a slum because he cannot imagine what is meant by an offer of a holiday at the sea. We are far too easily pleased.[14]

We must realize, once and for all, that wanting to fulfill our ultimate desires and seeking the rewards God offers us are not anti-Christian. What is anti-Christian is the self-centeredness that's unconcerned about God and our

neighbor, and the preoccupation with the immediate fulfilling of desires that distracts us from finding our highest fulfillment in Christ. The person who gives life, money, and possessions to receive rewards from God—the greatest of which is to hear the resounding "Well done"—is one whose deepest thirsts will be eternally quenched by the Maker and Fulfiller of desire.

It is senseless to devote our lives to the "mud pies" of power, possessions, and pleasures of this world, when our Lord offers to us the power, possessions, and pleasures of the next world, our true home.

You're an investor? Great. Invest in what counts the most. You have the desire to succeed? Fine. Succeed in servanthood, in giving, in praying, in reaching out to the lost and needy. You have ambitions? Good. Make them kingdom ambitions. You have dreams? Wonderful. Trade in your short-term dreams for the eternal dreams of the risen Christ. Joy and rewards unimaginable will be yours.

Of investments they say, "If it sounds too good to be true, it probably is." But in the case of the amazing return we can get on investments in God's kingdom, it *is* true. God himself guarantees it.

DREAMS OF ETERNAL DIMENSIONS

Every year in Portland, Oregon, builders showcase a row of big, beautiful houses called the "Street of Dreams." Although the houses are fun to look at, I'm struck by how sad it would be to have a dream as small as one of those houses.

When I was a pastor, a wonderful couple came to my office and told me they wanted to be able to give more money to the church and to missions, but they couldn't if they were going to keep saving to build their dream house. They said, "We've always had this dream for a beautiful home in the country, and we can't seem to shake it. Is that wrong?"

I told them I thought their dream of a perfect home was from God. I think they were surprised to hear that. Then I said, "It's just that your dream can't be fulfilled here, in this world."

Our dream house is coming; we don't have to build it ourselves. In fact, we can't. Any dream house on earth will eventually be ravaged by time, floods, earthquakes, tornadoes, carpenter ants, or freeway bypasses. Who would want to divert kingdom funds to build a dream house on earth if they understood that either it will leave them or they will leave it? Instead, why not use our resources to send building materials ahead to the Carpenter, our Bridegroom, who this very moment is building our dream house in heaven?

Grasping the law of rewards requires that we think often and accurately about heaven.

Writing in 1649, Pastor Richard Baxter asked a probing question:

> If there be so certain and glorious a rest for the saints, why is there no more industrious seeking after it? One would think, if a man did once hear of such unspeakable glory to be obtained, and believed what he heard to be true, he should be transported with the vehemency of his desire after it, and should almost forget to eat and drink, and should care for nothing else, and speak of and inquire after nothing else, but how to get this treasure. And yet people who hear of it daily, and profess to believe it as a fundamental article of their faith, do as little mind it, or labour for it, as if they had never heard of any such thing, or did not believe one word they hear.[15]

May we joyously believe. And then may we live as if we believe! May we live today as people who know God is watching, inviting us to invest all that we are and have into his kingdom. May we live with heaven on our minds, joyfully believing that our God is the Rewarder of those who diligently seek him.

QUESTIONS AND ANSWERS ABOUT REWARDS AND GIVING

Since God is our Father, not our employer, can we really earn eternal rewards? Wouldn't that be putting God in our debt?

In his stewardship parables, Christ portrays God as our master, and us not merely as slaves but as employees who are entrusted with financial assets that we're called upon to invest. The money-owner then repays us according to how well we've done our job in investing his assets. If we've proven faithful, he puts us in charge of many things.

It is therefore incorrect to say, "God is our Father, not our employer." He is both. If I only think of God as my employer, this would be unbalanced. He is also my King, Father, owner, shepherd, and so forth. Christ is my Lord, bridegroom, friend, and brother. He is not one instead of the others; he is all at once. To say that God pays us, his servants, for our labors is not the whole picture, but it is certainly part of the picture.

Does this imply God is put in our debt? No. It is he—not us—who puts the value on our service. It is he, not us, who commits himself to repay our service to him. We make no demands on him. It would be blasphemy to do so. But he tells us that he keeps accounts and will repay us generously for our service.

Christ said, "But when you give a banquet, invite the poor. . . . Although they cannot repay you, you will be repaid at the resurrection of the righteous" (Luke 14:13-14). God says he himself will repay us. The word "repay" means that God chooses to put us, unworthy though we are, in a position to be paid back. It's his promise.

It is one thing for me to say, "God, if I give a cup of cold water in your name, you are in my debt to repay me." That would be wrong. But when God himself, by his own gracious decree, promises he will "repay" us, then by embracing that promise we are not presuming upon him but trusting him.

So if I give a cup of cold water, do I earn or deserve a reward? In one sense no. In another sense yes. God is not only gracious but just. He rewards us by grace but also in justice—a just God does not reward unless it is not only gracious but right for him to do so. When Christ says, "Well done my good and faithful servant," I think he will really mean, "You've done a good job and in doing so you have, by my grace, earned the reward which it pleases me to give you."

We are God's children but not only his children. We are also his servants and stewards, hired by him to do a job, examined by him as to the job we've done, and generously rewarded by him if we've done it.

What are we missing if we do not give, especially to the needy?

If we don't reach out in our giving, as individuals and as churches, we miss out on a central aspect of biblical teaching: God's deep concern for the poor and needy. It was said of King Josiah, "He defended the cause of the poor and needy, and so all went well. Is that not what it means to know me?" (Jeremiah 22:16).

We miss out on *Christlikeness,* because Christ is the ultimate giver (2 Corinthians 8:9). "Grace" is giving, and Jesus was full of grace and truth. Giving is an expression of his basic nature. We give because he first gave to us.

We also miss out on a *great privilege.* When the Macedonians were told they didn't need to give because they were so poor themselves, they "urgently pleaded . . . for the privilege" of giving to the needy (2 Corinthians 8:4).

We miss out on *blessing,* because Jesus said, "It is more blessed to give than to receive" (Acts 20:35).

We miss out on *evangelistic opportunities,* because so many of these come when we reach out to the poor. Jesus said people would know us by our love for one another. After explaining how the early church would sell their assets to give to the needy, Scripture tells us God added to the church's numbers daily (Acts 2:47). No wonder, since their radical concern for the needy could only be explained by a powerful work of God.

By failing to reach out to the needy, we miss out on *eternal rewards,* because Jesus said if we give to those who can't pay us back, God himself will pay us back by rewarding us in heaven (Luke 14:14).

How can pastors teach their congregations the art of joyful giving?

Paul said, "I have not hesitated to proclaim to you the whole will of God" (Acts 20:27). Because Scripture puts so much emphasis on stewardship, money management, and giving, pastors should feel compelled to teach on this subject. The fact that it is often abused by false teachers is all the more reason to address it in a biblical and Christ-centered way. Many pastors are self-conscious about addressing financial issues, lest it leave a bad impression with the church or visitors. Furthermore, incredibly, most Bible colleges and seminaries that prepare people for ministry offer no classroom instruction or in-depth discussion on stewardship and giving. Pastors need encouragement from their congregations to teach in this critical area.

There are two different ways for pastors to appeal to their people concerning giving: *Give because it will bring you joy,* and *give because it will bring you eternal reward.* In other words, don't just do it because it's right, but because it's smart and it will bring you joy.

Pastors can emphasize the truth that everyone benefits from giving. This includes the recipients, the givers, the church, and God, who gets the glory, as well as those who see it and are drawn to Christ (and the church) as a result.

There are other reasons for giving, including duty, but many people already know that. What they really need is something fresh and radical and motivating. That's exactly what Jesus offers in Matthew 6 when he calls us to store up our treasures in heaven. Each day of our lives, we can rejoice because we're moving closer to our treasures.

I encourage pastors to be generous givers themselves. If they're not, their words will ring hollow. Joyful giving is contagious. A giving pastor will infect others with enthusiasm about giving.

Is it always wrong to let others know how much we give financially to the Lord's work? If we say anything at all about what God is teaching us about our giving, does that mean we will lose our rewards? In the beginning of the Sermon on the Mount, Jesus centers on actions, but in Matthew 6 he goes directly to motives. He mentions three "acts of righteousness"—giving, prayer, and fasting—and says, "Be careful not to do your 'acts of righteousness' before men, to be seen by them" (v. 1). This is not a prohibition disallowing others to see or become aware of your giving, prayers, fasting, Bible study, missions work, and so forth. However, it is a commandment not to do these things *in order to* receive the recognition of men.

Jesus continues, "If you do [good things to win the approval of men], you will have no reward from your Father in heaven. . . . I tell you the truth, they have received their reward in full" (vv. 1-2). In other words, if we give in order to get praise from men, we'll get what we seek—a college wing named after us, our name inscribed on a brick, maybe a prominent position on a board or our name in the newspaper. But in getting what we seek we will lose what we should have sought, the only thing that ultimately matters and survives—the approval and reward of God.

Jesus then says, "But when you give to the needy,

do not let your left hand know what your right hand is doing, so that your giving may be in secret" (vv. 3-4). This is a figure of speech. That it cannot be literal is self-evident—a hand has no ability to know anything, and a person has only one center of knowing, the brain, which knows what both the right and left hands are doing. A person can't throw a switch so he doesn't know he is giving.

So what does Jesus mean? Do your giving quietly and unobtrusively. Give in a spirit of humility and simplicity, as a private act of worship. Don't make a big production out of it, either before people or in the privacy of your own heart.

But there's another side to this issue. Often Matthew 6 is used as a proof text arguing that it is always wrong for others to know we have given. This is not true to the context. A mere ten minutes earlier in the same sermon, Jesus had said to his listeners, "Neither do people light a lamp and put it under a bowl. Instead they put it on its stand, and it gives light to everyone in the house. In the same way, let your light shine before men, that they may see your good deeds and praise your Father in heaven" (Matthew 5:15-16).

Clearly there is a time and a manner to appropriately share with others—to God's glory, not ours—information concerning our growth and experiences in relation to good works, including giving, praying, and fasting.

Acts 2 tells of Christians selling possessions and giving to the needy. Did people know who had done this? Acts 4:36-37 tells us that Barnabas sold a field and brought the money to the feet of the apostles. If Barnabas was looking for the reward of men, his motive was wrong. But it is impossible that it was wrong that others were made aware of his gift—because it's God's Word itself that tells us!

Does public recognition tempt people to give for the wrong motives? Absolutely. Ananias and Sapphira are examples. But the possible abuse of something doesn't nullify its legitimacy. The body of Christ can benefit from seeing open models of generous giving, and the world can benefit from seeing at the very least the corporate generosity of the church, as an attractive witness to the grace of Christ. The risks of disclosing someone's giving are sometimes outweighed by the benefits of disclosure.

The body of Christ needs to let its light shine before men, and we need models for the exercise of obedience and of the gifts. We dare not let the risk of our pride keep us from faithfully disclosing God's work in this area of our lives. That's why in the church we need to take the risk of openly telling stories of what God has done for us in the arena of giving. In fact, what may force me to swallow my pride more than anything is talking about giving when I run the risk of looking like I'm patting myself on the back. To vulnerably express to others where I am in my giving pilgrimage can be an act of humility.

I shouldn't brag about my Bible study or prayer or evangelism or giving, but I shouldn't cover it up, either. It's easier for people in our churches to follow footprints than commands. If we aren't willing to openly and humbly discuss giving, how can we expect to raise up givers? We can only be spurred on by what we can see.

One of many who have inspired my giving was R. G. Letourneau. An inventor of earthmoving machines, Letourneau reached the point of giving 90 percent of his income to the Lord. As he put it, "I shovel out the money, and God shovels it back—but God has a bigger shovel." I consider his example as precious as the prayer example of George Mueller. But had these men not told their stories, you and I would be unable to glorify God concerning them . . . and unable to follow their examples.

Once I've decided to give, how do I decide where to contribute money? How can I be sure that the money I'm giving away will be used with integrity?
Before giving to an organization, ask these questions:

- ✛ Is the ministry Christ centered and biblically sound?
- ✛ Do its leaders have integrity, character, purity, and humility?
- ✛ Are systems and structures in place to keep the organization accountable for funds received and spent?
- ✛ Does the staff demonstrate a servant-hearted concern for those to whom they minister?
- ✛ How clear and strategic are this organization's goals, objectives, and tactics, and how effective is it in carrying them out?

✛ How much money does the organization spend on overhead expenses and fund-raising, and how much on actual ministry? (Overhead expenses are legitimate—the question is how much.)

✛ Is this ministry pervaded by a distinctly eternal perspective on life, ministry, and resources?[16]

The organization's Web site or informational material may give you these answers. In addition, talk personally with members of the organization or others who are familiar with it. Visit the organization if possible to see its work firsthand.

Are we rewarded in heaven for leaving money to Christian ministries when we die?

Hebrews 9:27 says, "It is appointed for men to die once, but after this the judgment" (NKJV). We will be rewarded for what we actually do on earth. I think that leaving instructions for what others are to do with what we leave behind is not the same as what we do while we're still alive.

Would Jesus have pointed to the woman who gave away her last two coins in the same way if she had died that day and left those same two coins to the temple charity in her will? I don't think so. Would he be pleased that she left the coins in her will, as opposed to wasting them? Sure. But I don't think the reward would be comparable.

I think God rewards faith and sacrifice. It takes no faith or sacrifice to leave stuff behind when you die, since hanging on to it isn't an alternative. Giving is choosing to part with something, while leaving is simply controlling the destination of what you couldn't hold on to.

Now, we will all leave something behind, and certainly it is good to leave substantial portions to the church and to Christian ministries. I simply don't think we should consider this a substitute for true giving, which is done while we are still alive and when we still must trust God to provide.

For more information on giving and eternal rewards, see the author's books *Money, Possessions, and Eternity* (Carol Stream, Ill.: Tyndale House Publishers, 2003) and *The Treasure Principle* (Sisters, Ore.: Multnomah Publishers, 2001), or his ministry Web site, www.epm.org.

ENDNOTES

[1] A. W. Tozer, "The Transmutation of Wealth," in *Born after Midnight* (Harrisburg, Pa.: Christian Publications, 1959), 106.

[2] John White, *The Cost of Commitment* (Downers Grove, Ill.: InterVarsity Press, 1976), 47.

[3] A. W. Tozer, "The Transmutation of Wealth," 107.

[4] John Bunyan, as quoted by Bruce Wilkinson, "Walk Thru Eternal Rewards" seminar and notebook (Atlanta, Ga.: Walk Thru the Bible Ministries, 1987).

[5] Charles Edward White, "Four Lessons on Money from One of the World's Richest Preachers," *Christian History* 19 (Summer 1988): 21.

[6] Randy Alcorn, *The Treasure Principle: Discovering the Secret of Joyful Giving* (Sisters, Ore.: Multnomah, 2001), 13.

[7] Randy Alcorn, *In Light of Eternity: Perspectives on Heaven* (Colorado Springs, Colo.: WaterBrook, 1999), 1–3.

[8] C. S. Lewis, *The Problem of Pain* (New York: Macmillan, 1948), 115.

[9] A. W. Tozer, "The World to Come" in *Of God and Men* (Harrisburg, Pa.: Christian Publications, 1960), 127, 129–30.

[10] John Bunyan, "The Resurrection of the Dead, and Eternal Judgment," http://philologos.org/__eb-jb/Resurrection/dead05.htm

[11] I am indebted here to some insights on reward shared by Bruce Wilkinson in a one-day gathering for Christian leaders at Western Seminary in 1987.

[12] John Bunyan, "Paul's Departure and Crown," www.johnbunyan.org/text/bun-paul.txt

[13] William Wilberforce, *Real Christianity* (Portland, Ore.: Multnomah, 1982), 65.

[14] C. S. Lewis, *The Weight of Glory* (New York: Macmillan, 1980), 17–18, 3–4.

[15] Richard Baxter, "The Saints' Everlasting Rest," in *The Practical Works of Richard Baxter* (Grand Rapids, Mich.: Baker, 1981), 39–40.

[16] Randy Alcorn, "Nineteen Questions to Ask before You Give to Any Ministry," www.epm.org/givquest.html.

THE LAW OF REWARDS AND ITS EIGHT PRINCIPLES

While our faith determines our eternal destination, our behavior determines our eternal rewards.

Reward Principle #1: Giving brings greater blessing than receiving.

Reward Principle #2: When we invest money now in God's kingdom, we will receive great rewards later in heaven.

Reward Principle #3: God offers us rewards that are eternal, imperishable, and inexhaustible.

Reward Principle #4: When we see our lives through the lens of eternity, our attitude toward wealth will change drastically.

Reward Principle #5: Obeying God is not only right, it's smart. It will always pay off in the end.

Reward Principle #6: We will have differing levels of reward in heaven, depending on our actions and choices on earth.

Reward Principle #7: Desiring rewards is a proper motivation for serving Christ.

Reward Principle #8: We are not to be motivated primarily by earthly power, possessions, and pleasures, yet we are offered all three in heaven if we invest now in God's kingdom.

*Visit www.christianbookguides.com for a
discussion guide and other book-group resources
for* The Law of Rewards

ABOUT GENEROUS GIVING

Studies show that U.S. Christians give proportionately less today than they did during the Great Depression.

Generous Giving is a nonprofit educational ministry that seeks to encourage givers of all income levels—as well as ministry leaders, pastors, teachers, and professional advisors—to fully understand and embrace what it means to live generously according to God's word and Christ's example. It was launched in 2000 by the Maclellan Foundation, a fifty-year leader in Christian grant-making, to stir a renewed commitment to generosity among Christians. *Our mission is to motivate followers of Christ toward greater biblical generosity.* We envision the hearts and minds of God's people transformed for revolutionary giving.

We offer an array of practical tools such as books, study guides, quarterly briefings, eNewsletters, and an exhaustive online library of news articles, statistics, Bible studies, streaming media, and Scriptures and sermons on generosity. We also sponsor large and small gatherings, in a safe environment free from the pressure of solicitation, where givers can hear inspiring stories of men and women who have experienced financial freedom through the joy of giving.

We also host the *Generous Giving Marketplace,* a

Web site that brings givers and ministry opportunities together (www.GGMarketplace.org). This is a one-of-a-kind classified listing of hundreds of funding opportunities posted by scores of Christian ministries.

See that you also excel in this grace of giving.
—2 CORINTHIANS 8:7, NIV

For more information about Generous Giving, we invite you to contact:

Experience the Joy.

Generous Giving, Inc.
One Fountain Square, Suite 501
Chattanooga, TN 37402
(423) 755-2399
www.GenerousGiving.org

More Generous Giving books from Tyndale . . .

Secrets of the Generous Life
Gordon MacDonald
ISBN 0-8423-7385-3

In this book of inspiring and thought-provoking reflections, best-selling author Gordon MacDonald reveals the secrets of joyful, generous living and explains why a generous lifestyle is such an accurate measure of one's soul.

Generous Giving is not a publicly supported charity and does not solicit funds or allow solicitation at any of its events.